marching to a different drum

successful learning for all kids

marching to a different drum

successful learning for all kids

ARTHUR P. ATTWELL, Ed.D.

WINEPRESS WP PUBLISHING

ISBN 1-57921-480-0
Library of Congress Catalog Card Number: 2002107011

ABOUT THE AUTHOR

Arthur P. Attwell, Ed.D., is professor of education and head of the Childhood Education Department at Nyack College—New York City, author, national consultant, conference and motivational speaker, and minister. He is a former elementary and middle school classroom teacher with inner city, suburban, and rural schools, school district administrator, and state university education professor. His areas of expertise are brain-mind research, learning styles, and classroom applications for all academic areas.

Dr. Attwell has presented hundreds of workshops and seminars to educational cooperatives, public and Christian schools, homeschool teacher groups, churches, and communities throughout much of the United States. He also provides free clinical services for children and adults with reading or learning difficulties.

Dr. Attwell currently resides in the Hudson River Valley region of New York, where he enjoys writing, speaking, and working with youth, schools and homeschool groups, and community-educational partnerships for youth and adult outreach.

To children everywhere, may I always continue to learn from you.

"One hundred years from now it won't matter what size bank account we had, or the value of our home, or even the kind of car that we drove; what will matter is the difference that we made in the life of a child." Anonymous

CONTENTS

Marching to a Different Drum 11

Acknowledgements 13

Foreword 15

Preface 19

1. Brain-Mind Research: Six Keys to Optimize Learning for
   Kids 23

2. Key 1: Talents—Unfolding Natural Abilities 31

   Strategies and Activities 39

3. Key 2: Love—Providing a Nurturing Classroom 47

   Strategies and Activities 51

4. Key 3: Peace—Relaxing the Learning Environment 65

   Strategies and Activities 69

5. Key 4: Trust—Developing a Trusting Learning Climate 81

   Strategies and Activities 83

6. Key 5: Joy—Motivating Kids' Learning 95

    Strategies and Activities 99

7. Key 6: Commitment—Helping Kids Develop
    Perseverance 125

    Strategies and Activities 127

8. In Closing: Soaring as a Butterfly....................................... 137

"We Haven't Turned Out Yet" 139

Nutritious "Play Dough"! 141

MARCHING TO A DIFFERENT DRUM

In Trina Paulus' delightful story, *Hope for the Flowers*, two former caterpillars, Stripe and Yellow, saw the futile climbing of millions of caterpillars following one another as they climbed without destination or understanding. Stripe and Yellow had discovered the true transformation as butterflies. They had heard a different drum and wanted to share it with others.

ACKNOWLEDGEMENTS

I would like to express my deepest appreciation to three persons who devoted themselves to the thorough reading of this manuscript and provided many thoughtful suggestions and insights: My adopted mom, who has taught me unconditional love, a deeper walk with God, and how to look beyond all that I see, all by example; Dr. Robert Moore, beloved colleague, who has extended the hand of unconditional friendship and brotherhood; and Mr. Bernhard Storch, my friend and adopted grandfather, who has shared the importance of having the courage of one's convictions, no matter what the cost.

All three individuals understand the price of sacrifice in their own lives and the importance of teaching children to become all that they can be for God as they reach out to others in this world.

There is another group to which I am indebted: all the children and students with whom I have had the privilege of working over the many years, who have taught me so very much.

FOREWORD

TO TEACHERS, PARENTS, AND

OTHERS WHO WORK WITH KIDS

. . . unless you become as a child . . .

Luke 7:18

This book is about kids—how each child is individually made, each with his or her own unique style of learning. Yet more importantly, it's about *how* kids learn, *what* they enjoy doing, and *how* they see the world about them. But of even greater importance is the spiritual development of our children as it relates to their learning and growth. One cannot be separated from the other.

Not only is each child a gift from God, each child is given a special anointing to fulfill God's plan for his or her life. For no child is an accident or mistake on the part of God, each one is uniquely created and has a definite purpose in God's plan. And this is where teachers and parents come in: It becomes their moral and spiritual responsibility to carefully guide children entrusted to them, develop them into successful learners, and help them become all that God has purposed for their lives. We are biblically instructed to do this and we are held accountable. Therefore, this book attempts to present an instructional approach that is educationally sound, yet scripturally premised. There must be a balance.

In order to effectively teach our children, we must remember what it was like to be a child ourselves. Do not be offended, but unless you are willing to look at this book through the eyes and heart of a child, you might as well return this book to the store where you bought it or give it to someone who really will read it from a child's perspective. For until we can identify directly and honestly with our kids, we cannot effectively teach them. Just as the little boy in *The Polar Express* who still could hear the ring of Santa's sleigh bell when he became older, many adults could not. And still cannot.

We need to remember the laughter, imagination, and wonderment of our youth, and appreciate, enjoy, and value what is within our children. We must put aside our adult logic and reasoning, all the "pressures" of adulthood and their accompanying responsibilities and challenges, and learn to become childlike with our own children; for unless we do, we will fail them.

Have you ever seen the eyes of children when they see their first snowfall, taste real outdoor snow cones covered with fresh maple syrup, slide down a snow-covered hill on a sled or inner tube, throw snowballs, or make a snowman similar to Billy's in *Family Circus* that is "bigger than anything around?" Or how about witnessing the birth of baby puppies or ducklings that are just beginning to hatch—the joy of seeing life as an expression of God's creation? Perhaps it's riding a bike for the first time, painting a picture that is unlike any other, creating a "castle" with twigs, sand, pebbles, and leaves, or singing outdoors with butterflies that even dance in the air to the melody. Whatever it is, this wonderment— a moment of raptured joy—cannot be ignored. It must be cherished and savored.

The way that we wanted our own teachers and parents to approach us with our learning when we were in school is the very way that we are to approach learning with our own children: to provide them an unconditional, unwavering love; give them the emotional and physical security they need; share with their joy and exuberance with their discoveries; help them to identify and develop their talents; patiently nurture and encourage them through their growth and learning process in the face of all their challenges; and share alongside them the encouragement, tears, sufferings, and triumphs through it all.

Learning does not come easily for most kids, and each of us can remember back to our own childhood those subjects, concepts, or skills that had become obstacles to us and the inner frustration and discouragement that followed. I recall my first-grade year in Inglewood, California, when all of my classmates were dismissed for recess twice daily, yet I was the one who remained in class during each recess period practicing the correct writing of my lower-case *bs* and *ds*. My teacher wondered aloud if I ever would learn. Interestingly, I still have occasional trouble correctly writing them, even with an earned doctorate.

By the same token, effective teaching can be demanding for those who are willing to take the time to understand how each child learns best. We are to search all avenues to discern our children's learning strengths and then provide them every opportunity to succeed. What is important to realize is this: All kids in one way or another, and at one level or another, can become successful learners. It remains our responsibility to allow them to become as such.

What this book provides are the various ways kids learn best and the six-key foundation that is needed to provide successful learning for all children. Whether a child is learning disabled, labeled at-risk, gifted/talented, or "average" (I've never met an "average kid" in all my years in education!) is incidental, the strategies and approaches presented in this book will be of benefit to each one. Regardless of each child's areas of strengths and "challenges," this book shows how to provide successful, meaningful learning experiences for all kids and enable them to become all that God has intended for them to be.

Dr. Arthur Attwell, Chair and Professor
Department of Childhood Education
Nyack College–New York City
Summer, 2002

PREFACE

To frame the focus of this book, and my conviction as to its importance, I would like to invite you to join me in a wooded area of upstate New York.

A small child finds a tiny bundle of fur, with many, many legs, crawling on the ground. He reaches down to pick it up—its feet tickle him as it crawls about his hand and arm. Not wishing to lose this little creature—with a name so long he cannot pronounce—he places it into a jar and sets it on his bedroom nightstand.

Several hours later, his mother observes the trapped caterpillar and asks her son what he plans to do with it.

"Oh, I'm gonna keep it with me all the time, and we're gonna be good friends."

His mother, with all her wisdom and love, asks him if he knows what a caterpillar becomes when it has freedom. After she explains, she leaves the young boy and enclosed caterpillar alone. The boy realizes that for this ball of fur to become a glorious butterfly, he must take it outside and release it.

A few days later, the boy watches the caterpillar climb a sheltered wall outside, suspend itself from an overhead rafter, and tightly wrap itself into a cocoon. Throughout all this wonderment over the next week, he sees a majestic, yellow-and-black morning glory emerge from its cocoon and suddenly leap into the sunlight.

Soon it dances before him, alights on his outstretched hand, and tickles his finger with its proboscis, before flying back into the sky.

"Mommy, you're right. It's a beautiful butterfly—and its home is the whole outdoors."

In many ways, children are caterpillars, pupae within their cocoons, or butterflies—some have no idea who they are or where they're going, others have not discovered their abilities, while a few are soaring confidently high above; there are many caterpillars which have been squashed, as well as those pupae that remain trapped within their cocoons, waiting to be released. But one fact remains: All children have the potential to become butterflies. This is God's desire for all His children.

These butterflies are as unique as snowflakes, for no two are alike—they vary in size, shape, and color. Butterflies are nothing more than the horizons that exist within each child. For some children, their horizons are extended and virtually the sky's the limit; whereas for others, their horizons are limited, and yet, for some, nonexistent, in their own eyes. It becomes our primary goal to enable children to discover the butterflies within them and release them, for in so doing, we are helping them to become all that they can be. A fact of nature, though, must be realized: If the cocoon is not opened by the butterfly itself through struggle, but by another, its wings never will become strong enough for it to fly, and it soon will die.

The way by which this can be achieved is to provide kids two things: a learning environment that sets the stage for optimal learning growth and an instructional approach that allows kids to learn *their* way. Unless these two factors are in place, children's learning potential will never be fully realized.

This book provides the latest brain-mind research findings in simplified step-by-step fashion for teachers and parents who have children in school. The instructional approaches presented are appropriate for all children, regardless of individual learning challenges. Activities and strategies that are shaped address all age levels, incorporate all learning styles, and are adaptable to any Christian or public school, or homeschool curriculum. It is hoped that classroom teachers, parents, and others who work with kids will experience the same measure of success that others and I have had with these approaches. The kindled eyes, alone, of your children will be reward in itself.—APA

1

Brain-Mind Research: Six Keys to Optimize Learning for Kids

All the world's most precious treasures lie quietly in the mind of a child.

Anonymous

Kids are like gifts—the outside wrapping doesn't reveal what's inside. They all have abilities wrapped within, but some are able to open their packages sooner than others; and there are those who never have their packages completely opened. It is only when we allow, encourage, and wisely guide our children that their abilities can emerge to their fullest. And this takes place when we teach kids in a way that they individually can learn best. As we carefully reach inside them to help guide their learning, we find our real reward as we watch their learning begin to soar.

What we must realize is this: No two children learn alike. For some, learning comes easily; whereas for others, learning difficulties become obstacles to overcome. These can take the form of an emotional learning "block," a resistance to a particular instructional approach that does not fit the individual learning style, or an actual learning disability or inhibiting condition (attention deficit hyperactivity disorder, for example). Whatever the case may be, a challenge is posed to the teacher or parent, which becomes an instructional challenge that needs to be resolved. Not all children are "problem" (or challenged) learners, but all children at one time or another face learning challenges.

I have worked with many parents and teachers, laughed with them and cried with them, as we faced the struggles of learning for some of their children. For some parents, their concerns have been in specific areas, such as a daughter having difficulty with fractions and simply "can't see it." Others have been broader, as in the case of an eight-year-old son who was a nonreader. This is why I have written this book: Learning does not come easily for all kids and there are those times that we as teachers and parents feel that our backs are against the wall with no way out. And this is where this book can provide insight into such challenges and share ways to enable children to become successful learners, both from a practical and Christian perspective.

Brain-Mind Research Findings

There is so much that we do not know or understand about the human mind. And yet with the little that we do know about it, brain-mind research shows us that in order to optimize learning, we need to incorporate whole-brain learning. This is not confined to left-and right-brain hemisphericity (popularly referred to as *left-brain/right-brain thinking*) or the three basic learning modalities— *auditory* (listening), *visual* (seeing) and *kinesthetic* (touching/ movement). Research findings go well beyond that to Howard Gardner's *multiple intelligences*. Although Gardner's book, *Frames of the Mind: Multiple Intelligences,* was published from a secular perspective, his findings actually reveal the majesty and perfection of God's creation. We are discovering more and more of the mathematical precision of outer space; the same application holds true for the "perfectness" of our inner space—our mind. How wondrously we are created!

What is tragic is that we have all this information at our fingertips, yet so little is done in the majority of our nation's classrooms (public, private, or Christian) and home schools to capitalize on this wealth of knowledge and maximize the learning potentials of our children. Understanding how individual children learn enables us to more effectively teach and help them to climb to new plateaus. Further, this knowledge helps unlock the abilities that lie within each child. Now if only we would put this knowledge to practice.

God has placed specific abilities within each person, regardless of the challenges or disabilities the person faces. In order to bring forth these abilities to their fullest, we must first provide opportunity for them to flourish. We do so by teaching our children according to their individual learning styles.

Developing the mind and developing abilities, therefore, go hand-in-hand. But unless we provide learning experiences that stimulate whole-brain learning, opportunity for abilities to be identified might otherwise never materialize. A potentially gifted artist, if not given opportunity to allow her abilities to be observed, may go years never having this ability developed. Perhaps it may be those who can provide us an even greater enrichment and celebration in music, medicine, mathematics, teaching, writing, or even leadership.

We have found this to be the case with such persons as Thomas Edison, Albert Einstein, Eleanor Roosevelt, Winston Churchill, Booker T. Washington, Sojourner Truth, Helen Keller, and the list goes on. All of these noted people in history had learning problems of one type or another. And it was only when they were taught in the way that they learned best that they actually began to grow and excel. Who knows what might have happened had they not been taught *their* way? One thing is for certain: our world would have been deprived of all that each of these individuals had to offer.

The same principle applies to our children. The possibilities are endless, yet they remain *ended* if not allowed to first begin. And this is where we come in: We need to look for those abilities that lie within our children. The only way, though, that we can discover what treasures lie within each of our children is to provide opportunity for them to be revealed by teaching across the brain. Once learning strengths are identified and special learning styles addressed, abilities will emerge and begin to flow. Not only will children have greater success in learning, they also will have the joy of watching their abilities unfold and benefit others.

Teaching to the child's learning style is one side of the coin; the other side is providing those conditions within the learning environment that optimize children's learning experiences. All together, six keys are needed to ensure quality learning: (1) teaching to the child's individual learning styles; (2) providing a nurturing classroom climate; (3) relaxing the learning environment; (4) ensuring a safe and trusting atmosphere; (5) providing motivating learning experiences; and (6) helping children develop learning perseverance.

At this point, I would like to share stories of three children, with whom I have worked, who experienced learning success once the model that is presented in this book was applied.

Leonard's Story

Leonard was a learning-disabled fourth-grader with cerebral palsy. His gait was awkward and he drooled when he spoke. Leonard constantly dropped things—school supplies and lunch trays—wherever he walked. Smaller than most fourth-graders, he was timid and often socially isolated at the start. In effect, he was perceived by many of his classmates as a *social outcast.*

Learning had been a struggle for him. In fact, several former teachers had given him only "easy" tasks to accomplish, basically, because they didn't want to be inconvenienced and wanted to keep him "busy." Leonard was regarded as "very slow" by some and lazy by others. To some extent, the laziness was true—he had learned to manipulate the learning situation and use his physical and mental challenges to get him out of work.

His parents decided to transfer him to a Christian school in their community that specialized in serving children with learning difficulties. Although the long-range picture for him appeared "hopeless," there was a noticeable glint in his eyes during certain learning activities; projects that he developed revealed visual-spatial and musical-rhythmic learning modality strengths. Surprisingly, a bodily-kinesthetic learning modality strength also was noticed, in spite of his motor disability. (These and other learning styles are fully explained in chapter 2.)

Once math lessons by his teachers were presented to him in terms of these modality strength areas, Leonard began to catch on. Soon, he began to develop into a top flight learner in math. Older students joined in peer tutoring. He learned geometry by drawing concepts in shaving cream smeared on the table, putting formulas to music, and imagining applications.

Leonard was learning to learn *his* way. Soon his talents began to emerge and classmates saw the results of a shared effort: Leonard was becoming a successful learner in his studies and other abilities began to emerge, drawing for one.

CHARLENE'S STORY

Let me share another child's story that illustrates how appropriate teaching can turn a learning situation around. This particular story has a public school classroom setting and is appropriate for this book.

It was the start of a new school year. Charlene was a new transfer to the sixth-grade class. She had a poor self-image and had been constantly ridiculed by her parents. Coupled with this was a poor academic track record from her former school district that had extended for five years. Achievement test scores for her fifth-grade year showed her to have a composite performance grade level of low second-grade, with a composite reading score of only third-grade level, and yet she was assessed at a ninth-grade instructional reading level by her new teacher. Teacher comments that had previously been entered into her cumulative records could be summed into one statement: low ability.

As her teacher, I later discovered that she had been told by a former teacher that she was *slower* than her classmates and not to expect too much. Up to that year, she hadn't.

As the days passed by, it was observed that she had pronounced learning strengths: Her verbal-linguistic, visual-spatial and intrapersonal abilities seemed to jump out, along with her interest areas. Adapting the instructional approach to accommodate her learning styles and interests, Charlene began to shine academically and eventually was placed into the school's gifted and talented program.

Michael's Story

I first met Michael and his family seven years ago. His special education teacher, who had him in a daily pullout program from his regular class, had contacted me to see if I would be willing to do a reading and learning styles assessment with Michael, who apparently had pronounced reading problems and general learning difficulties.

Michael was a bright, eager child who, at the age of seven, was aware of his own learning problems and inability to keep up with other classmates. Simply put, his mind worked differently than minds of most kids.

Working with Michael, I found that he was tired of testing situations and being the center of everyone's concern, so our assessment session was a relaxed and fun experience for him. He had a strong receptive vocabulary that was well above his grade level, yet he was weak in word recognition and reading fluency. He also had a processing problem, especially with verbal sequencing, and he needed glasses. Michael's learning strengths were his bodily-kinesthetic and visual-spatial abilities.

Michael's parents were given some approaches to try at home, such as writing words on his back as he wrote them in shaving cream on the kitchen table, or writing words on index cards in colorful markers, then "tracing" them first with white glue and later retracing them with his finger once the glue had dried. His entire family developed imaginative stage plays with roles for each family member. Scripts were learned and acted out. Soon Michael's word recognition skills and oral reading fluency began to improve.

Also, the parents maintained a close relationship with their son's special education teacher and, with their combined efforts, saw a young boy develop into an honor roll student in his regular classes two years later!

Leonard's, Charlene's, and Michael's stories aren't isolated. In one way or another, there are many Leonards, Charlenes, and Michaels in conventional classrooms and home schools. Some are more severe; others have barely noticeable weaknesses. Exceptionalities (such as learning disabilities and attention deficit disorders), cultural and ethnic differences, language barriers, low self-images, and even learning boredom can become *at-risk* factors that span children from all backgrounds. It seems that without our discernment, concern, and appropriate teaching approaches, these kids have little chance for success.

ALL KIDS HAVE POTENTIAL

This brings us to how so many of us can fail to bring our children up to their true levels of potentiality. And this can only be done by teaching to children in the way that each individually learns best. What is fundamental is this: all children can learn. All children have God-given potentials that exist within them. And it is our responsibility to identify and nurture these potentials, and guide children toward their full attainment.

We need to reach all areas of the learning process—the curriculum, the environment, the teaching approach, and the child's individual learning styles. Such teaching isn't really new. The only problem is that it has been ignored by so many of us. One thing is certain, though, when we teach in this manner, growth in all areas is inevitable. Research findings continue to support this.

Using Leonard as an example, let's see the applications in his own life. Physical activity was incorporated into his learning activities. Some of Leonard's learning modality strengths were physical, in spite of his disability, and, once recognized, not only did his learning improve, but also his overall coordination, strength, and dexterity.

The mind is a complex organ; individual strengths and learning styles vary among children. Leonard's ability to visualize and learn spatially, as well as by colors, became evident. Once he learned to utilize these strengths, his learning focus became sharper, and his ability to grasp previously "unattainable" concepts came so easily.

Leonard's learning environment was stimulating, quietly interactive, and yet calm, to which he responded well. (Studies continue to reveal that a peaceful learning environment qualitatively promotes better learning.)

It seems, though, that the emotional area is so often overlooked by so many of us. Not only is this area essential, it intertwines closely with learning. Kids so desperately need the emotional encouragement, as well as unconditional acceptance and love to optimize their learning and overall development. Although Leonard did not have the emotional support or foundation he needed at school for the previous years, he did receive both from his parents and siblings at home. And this made a significant difference in his academic performance, his attitude toward himself and others, and his general outlook on life.

Interestingly, the approaches used with Leonard, Charlene, and Michael have been applied in a number of classroom and home settings. In each case, teachers and parents have shared with me that their children who had learning difficulties in various areas began to experience learning success, and those children for whom learning came easily began reaching even higher levels of achievement.

The chapters that follow address the six essential keys to successful learning, and provide down-to-earth explanations, condensed research findings, approaches and examples, and a variety of unique, effective learning activities and strategies that can be incorporated easily into any curriculum. Activities and strategies presented are "guidelines" that can be adjusted and adapted to fit any child or group of kids, setting, subject area, grade level, and classroom or home setting.

2

KEY 1: TALENTS—UNFOLDING NATURAL ABILITIES

The plan in the heart of a child is like a deep river; it takes a wise teacher to draw it out.

Adaptation of Proverbs 20:5

Alicia, it's right in front of you! How come you don't see it? Everybody else does!"

Her head slumps between her hands with elbows propped upon her desk. Tears begin to roll down all too familiar trails.

Not all children are able to see what we're trying to teach them. As a result, both teacher and child become frustrated. What research and best practices in education have revealed is that successful learning is directly linked to our instructional approach and our ability to tap into the children's individual learning styles.

COLORFUL PRISMS: DEVELOPING TALENTS IN CHILDREN

Each child's brain has its own combination of learning styles; no two children learn alike. Each brain is distinctly different and unique. There is no single learning style a child has, but rather each child possesses several (or more) areas of strength. And these vary from child to child.

In many ways, minds of children resemble a colorful prism: Each mind is reflective, multi-faceted, unique, and filled with abilities. For some children, unless their classroom teacher or parent provides learning experiences that address their specific learning styles, they may never "catch on" or excel to their potential. The problem that develops is when we teach a variety of children with one or two instructional approaches that reflect only one or two learning styles. What is then expected is for *all* children to understand what is being presented and perform identically. Unfortunately, this does not reflect reality.

Each child has a unique combination of learning styles, which not only is the first key for successful learning for that particular child, but also the vital key to unlocking the child's abilities. Not all children learn the same way; therefore, they should not all be taught the same way. What is needed is for us to identify each child's learning styles and adjust the instructional approach accordingly. As a result, not only will learning become more successful, but the child's abilities will emerge as well.

The section that follows presents the sum of brain-mind research in simple, easy-to-follow applications that can be used in any classroom or home setting or grade level.

BRAIN-MIND RESEARCH SIMPLIFIED

There are seven identified ability areas that comprise the human brain:

VERBAL-LINGUISTIC ABILITY

This is the ability to put thought into words and to use language in a variety of ways. We use this ability when we speak to each other, write in a journal, tell a story, create poetry, or simply write a letter. Analogies, metaphors, puns, and humor come into play.

Some Ways to Develop Verbal-Linguistic Ability:

- *Write poetry—haiku is excellent to begin with.*
- *Brainstorm ideas for a project, field trip, and so forth.*
- *Learn an interesting new word each day and practice using it.*
- *Play with words, using tongue twisters, puns, or nonsense rhymes.*
- *Play word games: crosswords, word jumbles, Scrabble, etc.*
- *Write or tell a sequel to a story.*
- *Keep a journal and record thoughts and feelings.*
- *Share ideas and opinions. Ask questions or engage in discussion.*
- *Develop a presentation on a topic of interest.*

MATHEMATICAL-LOGICAL ABILITY

This is most often seen in problem-solving situations and referred to as *scientific thinking*. It is the ability to see relationships, patterns, and think in imageless concepts. Such an ability is seen in its expression of Socratic questioning, ability to quantify or analyze things in the environment, setting up "what if" experiments, or playing games or solving brainteasers that require logical thinking.

Some Ways to Develop Logical-Mathematical Ability:

- *Create a sequence of numbers that have a hidden pattern.*
- *Develop a Venn diagram to find similar characteristics from two literary characters. (For example, compare shared traits of Stellaluna and The Ugly Duckling.)*
- *Find a relationship between ten randomly gathered objects. This can be done by size, use, color, etc.*
- *Develop a solution for a problem: the ozone layer, rainforest, or smog.*
- *Do mental mathematical computations.*

VISUAL-SPATIAL ABILITY

This is most easily seen in the active imaginations of children: having a pretend friend, playing school with stuffed animals, imagining oneself as a hero or heroine in a story, are but a few examples. Such ability enables kids to imagine a story they are writing, perform a gymnastics routine in their minds, play chess (and *see* the board several plays later), and turn a drawing into a real object.

Some Ways to Develop Visual-Spatial Ability:

- *Draw or doodle while listening to a story.*
- *Imagine oneself as a person from history or a Bible story and describe what it would be like to be that person.*
- *Express an idea or mood with markers, paints, or another art medium.*
- *Enjoy a jigsaw puzzle, maze, or another type of visual puzzle.*
- *Use a variety of colors—chalks, paints, markers—to teach another child a particular concept.*
- *Create a collage of magazine pictures that describes oneself, a sibling, or other family member.*

BODILY-KINESTHETIC ABILITY

This is the ability to perform things without a conscious effort: walk a balance beam, catch a baseball, and easily identify shapes or type on a keyboard with closed eyes. Mime, charades, dance, or other body movements can be used to express emotions or convey ideas. Learning is more easily grasped through a hands-on/movement approach, such as manipulatives to understand a particular math concept.

Some Ways to Develop Bodily-Kinesthetic Ability:

- *Use hand or facial gestures or other forms of body language, when conversing with someone or responding to a statement.*
- *Perform varied physical activities—mime, charades, dance, or movement—that correspond to a mood or opinion.*
- *Practice a new skill rather than hearing or reading about it or even seeing it in a demonstration.*
- *Act out a story.*

MUSICAL-RHYTHMIC ABILITY

Musical-rhythmic ability is the ability to use tones and rhythmic patterns of learning and expressing one's feelings. Particular sounds or musical-rhythmic patterns are associated with such moods as ecstasy and joy, sadness, fear, excitement, spiritual reverence, or even patriotism. Many children make tapping sounds or sing melodies while studying, working on a project, jogging, or writing a letter.

Some Ways to Develop Musical-Rhythmic Ability:

- *Observe and identify the natural rhythmic patterns of the environment: waves lapping on the shore, tree limbs swaying in the wind, rain beating on the rooftop, vocal or physical sounds of wildlife, and the like.*
- *Learn something new or memorize something already known through music by developing lyrics to a well-known tune. This can be done through jingle, chant, song, or rap.*
- *Tell a story and add various sound effects to the narration.*
- *At your table, tap out the rhythm of a poem as the teacher or classmate reads it.*

INTERPERSONAL ABILITY

This particular ability functions best through group discussion, projects, and other forms of cooperative learning. Such ability enables one to effectively read and relate to others, whether verbally or nonverbally, in mood, temperament, and intentions. Basically, it is the ability to discern or identify with another. Empathy and sensitivity to another are present—a child is able to "stand in another's shoes," so to speak.

Some Ways to Develop Interpersonal Ability:

- *Share a problem that needs solving—whether mathematical, physical, or emotional—with another.*
- *Practice listening intently to another person and stay focused on what that person is saying. Ask follow-up questions; paraphrase what the other person says.*
- *Teach a skill or concept to another.*

INTRAPERSONAL ABILITY

This ability enables a child to be introspective and self-reflective—it is a sense of deep individuality. Such persons are able to step back and watch themselves, as though looking from the outside through a window into what lies inside. Only humans have this capacity: a deeper awareness of self, feelings, thinking processes, and intuition, as well as a deeper spiritual awareness.

Some Ways to Develop Intrapersonal Ability:

- *Take time for quiet, personal reflection. This can be done through a reflective journal or diary of feelings, insights, and thoughts.*
- *Pretend to be an outsider looking in, observing thoughts, feelings, and moods. Notice patterns that develop with anger, worry, playfulness, joy, or peace. In short, develop an understanding of self.*
- *Develop a special hobby and become immersed in it.*

All kids have each of these abilities to varying degrees. These essentially translate into learning styles—that is, in order for kids to learn best, we teach to their strongest ability areas.

At this point, we are brought to a very real question that could become quite overwhelming: How do I identify and address the unique styles of each of my children? The answer is quite simple: At first, use an instructional approach that accommodates all learning styles, as much as is possible. This way, all children benefit. Further, learning becomes stimulating, successful, and enjoyable. Although this takes a little more time in planning, preparation, and implementation, it pays off in the long run. *As children are exposed to a variety of learning modes, their strengths will become evident to the teacher or parent, who can then adjust the teaching approach to fit each child's learning strengths.* This develops into a win-win situation for all involved.

What we must always keep in mind is this: Kids think in the way that they learn best; therefore, as we see our children perform successfully with particular learning abilities, we need to provide them opportunities to learn using these learning abilities (or learning styles). This does not become a learning crutch (which would be a misnomer); instead, it puts kids on a "best foot forward" basis and gives them equal footing with other kids who may be utilizing more conventional modes of learning.

An example of this is a particular child who may not see how a triangle, regardless of its shape or size, has a sum total of 180 degrees for its three angles. Some kids will understand the logic of this principle when it is presented verbally or even visually, yet others may not. This is when we need to try other approaches, such as cutting out several differently shaped and sized triangles, as illustrated on the following page, tearing off the points of a triangle's three angles, and fitting together the cut portions of the three angles, which will form a half circle (or 180 degrees).

This is why teaching across the brain is so vital—so that we can identify and teach to our children's abilities that lie deeply within.

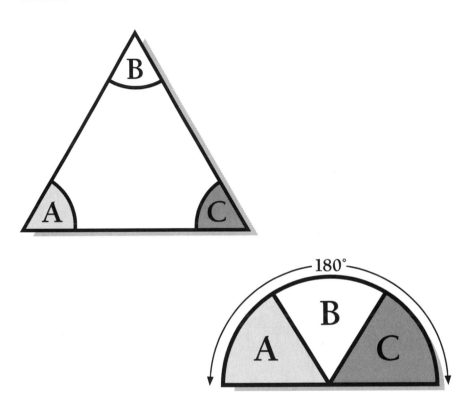

Sample strategies and activities to bring out children's natural abilities are presented in the next section.

Strategies and Activities

A child is not a vessel to be filled, but a lamp to be lighted.

Anonymous

Activity 1: Preschool/Kindergarten Lesson on Shapes

Let's move to a preschool/kindergarten lesson involving learning basic shapes: square, rectangle, triangle, circle. What might be suggested is to learn one shape per day and review all four on the fifth day.

1. Make a group square, rectangle, triangle, and circle. Kids form the shapes as an entire group, while holding hands. (bodily-kinesthetic, interpersonal)
2. Read or make up silly stories about the shapes. (verbal-linguistic)
3. Look for examples of the shapes in magazines, classroom environment, and outdoors. (mathematical-logical, visual-spatial)

4. Cut out shapes with construction paper, or draw and paint shapes. (bodily-kinesthetic, visual-spatial)
5. Sing a song about shapes. (There are a number of shapes songs available at teacher supply outlets.) (musical-rhythmic)
6. Dance to these songs and choreograph the movement to fit the "drawing" of the shape. (musical-rhythmic, bodily-kinesthetic)
7. Compare shapes to each other. Discuss differences. (visual-spatial, interpersonal)
8. Make shapes by using bodies while lying on the floor. It may take two, three, or even four children to "create" one shape. (bodily-kinesthetic, interpersonal)
9. Think of your favorite shapes and why you like them. (intrapersonal)
10. Create shapes with your own hands, using forefingers and thumbs. (bodily-kinesthetic)
11. Create shapes using rubber bands and geoboards. (bodily-kinesthetic, visual-spatial, mathematical-logical)

ACTIVITY 2: PRESCHOOL/KINDERGARTEN LESSON ON LEARNING NUMERALS (0–9)

Now, here's an example of a lesson involving the learning of numerals:

1. Create pictures using numerals. (visual-spatial)
2. Form numerals from colorful pipe cleaners. (bodily-kinesthetic)
3. Listen to Eric Carle's *The Very Hungry Caterpillar* and draw the numeral with crayon (or select the corresponding plastic numeral from a group of numerals) that represents the number of things eaten on that page of the story. (verbal-linguistic, visual-spatial, bodily-kinesthetic, mathematical-logical)

4. Form numerals with bodies while lying on the floor. (bodily-kinesthetic, interpersonal)
5. Standing in a group, form numerals as seen from overhead; draw the outline (trace around feet of group) with chalk on the carpet or erasable marker on linoleum. (bodily-kinesthetic, visual-spatial, interpersonal)
6. Form numerals with forefingers and thumbs. (bodily-kinesthetic)
7. Write numerals in shaving cream, finger paint, wet sand, or chocolate pudding. (bodily-kinesthetic)
8. Sing any number song while drawing or "presenting" (choice is up to child) corresponding numeral. (musical-rhythmic, visual-spatial)
9. Place plastic numerals in their proper order. (bodily-kinesthetic, mathematical-logical)
10. Sing a song with all ten numbers (such as "Ten Little Bluebirds"), while pointing to corresponding numerals. (musical-rhythmic, mathematical-logical)
11. Reflect on this question: Which is your favorite numeral? Why? (intrapersonal)
12. Create large "pillow numerals" for your class for children to prop themselves against while reading. (Patterns for pillow numerals are available from publishers of *Mailbox Magazine*.) (bodily-kinesthetic)
13. Dance in the form of the numeral. (musical-rhythmic, bodily-kinesthetic)
14. Perform fun and zany, yet easy, calisthenics or dance aerobics to the count. (musical-rhythmic, bodily-kinesthetic)
15. Write numerals in the air with the whole arm. (bodily-kinesthetic)

ACTIVITY 3: SAMPLE SPELLING APPROACH (GRADE LEVELS 3–6)

Provide each child the following learning experiences:

1. Say the word, break it into parts or syllables, then spell the word. (verbal-linguistic)
2. Find the numerical value of the word (a=1, b=2, c=3, etc.). (mathematical-logical)
3. Color code, imagine on a "mental sheet of paper," or illustrate the word. (visual-spatial)
4. Write word in shaving cream, finger paint, wet sand, or on fine-grain sandpaper. (Variation: For a tasty treat, give each child a sheet of waxed paper and a small can of precooked chocolate pudding. The approach is similar to using shaving cream. Smear chocolate pudding onto the waxed paper, and children can lick their fingers at each successfully spelled word.) (bodily-kinesthetic)
5. Clap word in syllables—all words have rhythm. Create a song, chant, or "rap" with spelling words. Rhythmic patterns also can be developed to remember each word. (musical-rhythmic)
6. Use a buddy system (see page 88). (interpersonal)
7. Reflect on the word and a creative way to use it, then enter the word into a journal or word bank (see page 62). (interpersonal)

This way, each child will have her specific learning styles addressed. Although a little more planning is involved, what is guaranteed is successful, quality learning for all kids where reteaching won't be necessary, only reinforcement of the concept through periodic review.

Activity 4: Two Sample Instructional Approaches for Individualized Learning Styles with Spelling or Vocabulary Words (grade levels PreK-6)

Let's assume that you have "locked in" on your children's learning styles. Taking two children at random, one with strong bodily-kinesthetic and visual-spatial learning strengths, the other with strong musical-rhythmic and interpersonal learning strengths, the approaches outlined below would be examples as how each child's learning new words could be approached. Using all of the techniques is not necessary. Several alone would suffice.

First child (bodily-kinesthetic and visual-spatial learning strengths):

1. Sculpt new words in nutritious, "play dough" (recipe on page 141).
2. Cut out (or draw) magazine pictures that depict or express the words.
3. Pantomime (mime) the words.
4. Make a hanging mobile with the new words.
5. "Write" new words in shaving cream, finger paint, chocolate pudding, or even wet sand.
6. Learn to "sign" the new words, using individual letters from the American Sign Language.
7. Create a "picture" with the new words (which form the outline of the picture).

Second child (musical-rhythmic and interpersonal learning strengths):

1. Create a song using the new words by humorously fitting them to a well-known tune and teaching the song to others.
2. Study the new words with a partner.
3. Develop a "rap" with the new words and share it with the class.

ACTIVITY 5: SAMPLE LEARNING EXPERIENCES WITH GEOMETRY—PARTS OF A CIRCLE (GRADES 4–8)

Let's apply this approach to upper elementary level geometry:
Geometric terms to learn: *circumference, radius, diameter, arc, chord.*

1. Discuss and write the meanings of each term in the child's own words. Root term meanings are explored and discussed. (verbal-linguistic)
2. Discover relationships in terms of meaning and *function* each geometric term has in relationship to the circle and other parts. (mathematical-logical)
3. Draw a circle, then color-code and label its parts. Encourage kids to close their eyes and imagine the five parts. (visual-spatial)
4. Construct a circle from any medium (clay, construction paper, wheat paste, wood, etc.), then design and label its parts. (bodily-kinesthetic)
5. Create and sing a song about circles (and their parts), or create a "rap" to help kids learn these terms. (musical-rhythmic)
6. Pair kids and have them reinforce the terms through cooperative learning. (interpersonal)
7. Provide quiet reflection time for kids to reflect on and write what they've learned in their journals. (intrapersonal)

All seven approaches can be incorporated easily into a single lesson. Teachers and parents, though, need to be cautioned not to be caught up with *quantity* of learning, but rather *quality* of learning. For it is when quality of learning takes place, reteaching concepts and skills is not needed, only occasional reinforcement. And this is where so many of us can fall short in teaching: We become so concerned about coverage of the entire curriculum that kids often are rushed through their learning and concepts never become cemented.

We continually must look at what we teach children through *their* eyes. And when we put this to daily practice and provide those much-needed quality learning experiences, kids become successful in their learning and horizons begin to expand even further.

ACTIVITY 6: MIDDLE SCHOOL SCIENCE/SOCIAL STUDIES LESSON (GRADE LEVELS 5–8)

Now, here's a sample science/social studies lesson on Arkansas and the bald eagle that incorporates all seven learning styles:

"Imagine yourselves atop a jutting, rocky precipice on Arkansas's Petit Jean Mountain, facing to the west from Mather Lodge. The sun is slowly ebbing into the horizon, splashing a striking display of colors across the western sky—fiery oranges, pinks, and magentas, then stark grays and violets.

"As you stand near the edge facing the sunset, you suddenly discover a lone eagle flying above the canyon walls that lie before you, with a winding river coursing its way about 700 feet below. You imagine what it might be like for the eagle in flight as it now spreads its wings behind and plummets down toward the river below in search of fish.

"You can imagine how the wind might feel blowing into the eagle's face . . . and the freedom that the eagle has in flight. . . ."

Seven 10- through 12-year-old children sit on the floor about the teacher, with their eyes closed, as she describes their adventure. Soft background forestral music accompanies the narration. They will be reading about the plight of the bald eagle in Arkansas, and their co-op homeschool teacher wants the topic to become very real to her kids. The children discuss what it might be like to be an eagle.

As the children read articles about Arkansas's bald eagles, they become more aware of migratory patterns, as well as predation of this distinctive member of the falcon family.

This is followed by a field trip to a location along Arkansas's Buffalo River—a protected area where migrating eagles find sanctuary. Kids bring sketch pads and are given quiet time to observe and sketch these majestic birds in flight, then they write personal observations and reflections in their journals.

Later, kids are able to touch a stuffed eagle that had died from electrical shock while perched on a power line and is now on display at a local museum.

A folk song depicting the plight of the bald eagle is sung and learned.

The teacher shares various references in the Bible pertaining to the eagle and its significance, as well as the eagle's symbolic meaning as our national emblem.

All learning styles of the brain are incorporated into this learning activity. And the children not only develop a greater understanding of the plight of the bald eagle, but also will better understand and remember what they learn.

Not all lessons can be taught with all seven learning styles; however, the learning styles that are incorporated will match at least one of a child's individual strengths.

3

KEY 2: LOVE—PROVIDING A NURTURING CLASSROOM

. . . and the greatest of these is love.

1 Corinthians 13:13

The following is a beautiful lesson on a nurturing classroom:

Tammy, a third-grader, had an extensive hearing loss and was self-conscious about her related speech problem. She recently arrived at a new school, and had made a friend in her class, but was teased by a few of the other kids because she "talked funny."

Tammy's classroom teacher wore an audiotron around her neck, which amplified the speech so that Tammy's hearing aid could pick up the teacher's speech. This way, Tammy could hear the teacher's instructions and most of the classroom conversation.

One day, Tammy was sad and down. Her teacher quietly spoke seven words into the audiotron that Tammy had years later shared with others. The seven words that made an impact on Tammy were simply, "Tammy, I think you are very special."

What children need—in fact, what we all need—more than anything else is unconditional acceptance and love, for this is the very foundation of all other needs. Research studies continue to provide evidence that a nurturing learning environment based on unconditional love is a foundational key to optimized learning and personal growth.

Teaching is not only a mind-to-mind connection, but also and more importantly, a heart-to-heart connection. Once this connection is genuinely made, kids begin to feel better about themselves, become more successful in their learning, develop more positive interpersonal relationships, and have an "I can do it" outlook.

Kids, as well as dogs, I tell my seminar participants and college classes, are perhaps the most discerning of psychologists, for they know when an honest, genuine love is present or absent. For love not only establishes foundational emotional roots, it also enables children to rise above and become butterflies and overcome what seem to be insurmountable barriers that confront them.

GRANDMA'S APPLE PIE

Grandma's apple pie is just what it implies: It's filled with tasty apples, spices, and love. As home-baked apple pies are filled with tasty morsels, children also need special inner ingredients full of hopes and dreams and love. For many young children, this inside picture is painted strong, positive, undaunted, and full of love. Sad to note, there are those whose critical, biting, cutting remarks leave a lasting impression upon children. Even worse are those children who receive little or no attention. Their internal value index plummets even lower. And their inside painted portraits are sad and empty.

Children need opportunities to grow in learning environments where they are appreciated and valued. Kids need to see and feel Christ's unconditional love and acceptance in action through their teachers, parents, classmates, and others, for this will enable children to mature academically, emotionally, and socially, resolve personal and interpersonal conflicts that may arise, and live a richer, more fulfilled life. It is this very key that is the greatest gift that we can give to our children: an unconditional, sacrificial love and acceptance that we allow to flow through us in our actions and responses to them.

WHAT RESEARCH SHOWS

Numerous research studies demonstrate the importance of emotional well being in the learning process. When kids have that security of unconditional love, they tend to perform better academically, realize healthier emotional growth, and are generally happier as individuals.

Activities and strategies that follow provide opportunities for fostering such a learning environment in the classroom or home by encouraging children to reach out to each other, as well as see and appreciate those good qualities that lie within themselves.

Strategies and Activities

We are shaped and fashioned by those who patiently love and inspire us.

Goethe

Body Awareness

There is a close relationship with body awareness and the development of a positive self-concept. Kids will make facial expressions before a mirror; they will watch how they walk, run, skip, hop, and crawl. Kids also watch others in a mirror, and they compare themselves to other kids. This awareness reinforces how they see themselves. Generally, kids see themselves in a positive light; sometimes, though, they may see themselves in a negative one.

The four activities that follow utilizing mirrors are varied and appropriate to almost any age group.

Activity 7: Mirroring

Grade levels:	PreK and up
Time involved:	10 to 20 minutes (depends upon activity)
Teacher's/parent's role:	Provide directions; join your children in the activity
Materials needed:	Varies according to activity

Learning styles: Visual-spatial, bodily-kinesthetic, verbal-linguistic, intrapersonal, interpersonal

Symmetry is a difficult concept for some children. Invite your children to stand before a full-length mirror and describe how the human body is symmetrical. Place a length of string or yarn down the length of a child's body, holding one end at mid-forehead (while standing behind the child) and letting the other end drop to the floor. (Older children can hold their own length of yarn—or kids can work in pairs—to find their own similarities.)

Point out the fact that one side of the yarn is almost a mirror image of the other side. Ask your children to find similarities.

"Oh, I get it! I have an ear on both sides of my head, and an eye. Also, I see . . ."

Kids find they're not perfectly symmetrical: one foot is generally a bit longer than the other; they may have a few more freckles on one cheek than the other. Regardless of differences, kids need to appreciate their uniquenesses.

ACTIVITY 8: SELF-SKETCH AND DESCRIPTIVE WARDROBE

Grade levels: PreK-6
Time involved: 10 to 20 minutes
Teacher's/parent's role: Provide directions; join your children in the activity
Materials needed: Sketch paper, marking pens, full-length mirror
Learning styles: Visual-spatial, verbal-linguistic, intrapersonal, interpersonal

As each child stands before a full-length mirror, ask her to draw or sketch herself. When she is finished, provide her a descriptive wardrobe: Write a number of positive *descriptors* that reflect her appearance, abilities, and personality. She may wish to add a few more.

Display your children's self-sketches and descriptive wardrobes on the classroom or homeschool bulletin board. Kids can never have too much positive reinforcement.

Extender: Each child will enjoy switching roles and asking another classmate or sibling to sketch her body on paper, and inviting all classmates or family members to write positive descriptors around the drawing.

For younger children, you can use a language experience approach (see page 59) and print positive descriptors each child gives to each classmate.

ACTIVITY 9: SELF-GROWTH CHARTS

Grade levels:	PreK-3
Time involved:	5 to 10 minutes
Teacher's/parent's role:	Provide guidance
Materials needed:	Tape measure, marking pen, chart (for recordkeeping), mirror
Learning styles:	Visual-spatial, bodily-kinesthetic, mathematical-logical, intrapersonal, interpersonal

Kids love to discover all they can about themselves: One such discovery is watching themselves grow up. An activity that lends to this interest is developing a self-record chart.

There are a number of things that can be recorded:

You can attach a length of measuring tape along the door jam of the classroom (these can be purchased in most department or school supply stores, and they come in an array of brightly illustrated tapes) and record your child's height every three or four months. Be sure to date each entry mark on the tape. (Some of your children may ask why they haven't grown much in a particular period of time. You reply that kids have different growth rates, and growth spurts can occur at different times. Let your child observe young caterpillars and adult butterflies—

each has an individual growth period, and each is beautiful and very special.)

Place a scale in your children's classroom and periodically record their weight. Keep a record by the scale. If at home, invite your child to weigh herself right before she goes to bed at night and again early in the morning. *Burning up calories* is a tough concept for younger kids, but is of interest to nine and ten-year-olds (this is the age when such specific questions begin to appear!).

Not only should there be a full-length mirror in the classroom, each child should have a full-length mirror in her bedroom. Kids are curious about themselves, whether it's noting physical changes, enjoying a charade or mime before the mirror, or observing personal appearance. Mirrors enable children to become more aware of themselves.

ACTIVITY 10: MIRROR, MIRROR ON THE WALL!

Grade levels:	PreK-2
Time involved:	Approximately 10 minutes
Teacher's/parent's role:	Facilitate; contribute positive comments
Materials needed:	Full- or half-length mirror
Learning styles:	Visual-spatial, verbal-linguistic, intra-personal, interpersonal

Your child looks into a mirror and selects one thing that he likes about himself. You then join in and share what you like about him. You look into the mirror and select one thing that you like about yourself. After you both have had a turn, the two of you briefly share about how it felt to have something nice to say about the other person, as well as to hear something nice about yourself spoken by the other person.

This is a wonderful opportunity for your child to feel good about himself.

Activity 11: Body Tracing

Grade levels: K-6
Time involved: 15 to 20 minutes
Teacher's/parent's role: Provide guidance
Materials needed: Large sheet of butcher paper, marking pen or crayon
Learning styles: Visual-spatial, bodily-kinesthetic, mathematical-logical, intrapersonal, interpersonal

Invite each child to lie down, with arms and legs slightly spread from the body, on a large sheet of white butcher paper (available at any supermarket meat department or teacher supply store). Using a marking pen or crayon, trace your child's body.

There are a number of things you can do with body tracing:

1. Mount your child's "body" on the home or classroom wall. Repeat the activity six months later and ask him to compare the new tracing with the earlier production. *Are there any differences in height, length of arms and legs, size of hands and feet, and so forth?*
2. Invite kids to write positive comments on his mounting profile. (Do body tracings for each classmate or family member.)
3. For older kids, they can measure their body's *perimeter* (the total distance around the profile of the body).
4. If your children are studying the concept of *area*, the body profile can be divided into one-inch (or one-centimeter) grids. Ask your children to estimate various sections of their bodies, then count the actual grids in each section. Your kids can estimate an *average body width* and multiply this with their *heights* to find an *estimated total body surface area* in square inches (or square centimeters).

ACTIVITY 12: SILHOUETTES

Grade levels:	PreK and above
Time involved:	30 minutes (may vary)
Teacher's/parent's role:	Provide directions, individual assistance
Materials needed:	Bright lamp or overhead projector, dark-colored construction paper, pencil, newspaper, marker, scissors, magazines, and masking tape
Learning styles:	Verbal-linguistic, visual-spatial, bodily-kinesthetic, intrapersonal (interpersonal included with cooperative learning)

Have each child sit approximately two feet in front of a sheet of newspaper taped to the wall. Position the lamp (or overhead projector) three feet from the child, and focus the lamp on the child's head to create a silhouette on the newspaper. Using a marker, outline each child's silhouette.

Once each child has been given his outlined silhouette, he cuts out the silhouette, places it on a sheet of dark-colored construction paper, then traces the silhouette with a pencil. The construction paper is then cut out and filled with a collage of magazine pictures or drawings, which describe him as he is, as well as what he wants to become. The collage is then displayed on the bedroom wall or classroom bulletin board.

Another approach is to cut out the actual silhouette (construction paper) and use a montage of colored tissue paper for a stained glass effect to fill in the cut out area of the remaining sheet of construction paper.

Your kids will appreciate the activity and the effect and will eagerly want to have them displayed.

ACTIVITY 13: ME MOBILE

Grade levels: PreK and above (parental assistance needed with younger children)

Time involved: 30 to 40 minutes (this activity can be divided into two 15 to 20 minute sessions)

Teacher's/parent's role: Explain purpose, provide direction, assist with activity

Materials needed: Magazine pictures, paper, yarn, markers or paint, wire clothes hangers, hole punch, gummed reinforcers (for picture holes to prevent tears), laminator or clear contact paper

Learning styles: Visual-spatial, mathematical-logical, bodily-kinesthetic, intrapersonal, interpersonal

Have your children select or draw pictures that best describe them. Laminate (or use clear contact paper on both sides) and punch holes into the pictures. Thread them with the yarn in an interesting way, and attach them to coat hangers to create a unique, balanced mobile.

Suspend each child's mobile from the home classroom (or child's bedroom) ceiling. Not only will it provide a distinctive decoration, she will be constantly "reminded" of her *specialness*.

ACTIVITY 14: THIS IS ME!

Grade levels: PreK-3

Teacher's/parent's role: Provide guidance, assist when needed

Materials needed: Paper, crayons or marking pens, hole punch, fastening brads or colorful yarn, magazines with colorful pictures

Learning styles: Verbal-linguistic, mathematical-logical, visual-spatial, intrapersonal, interpersonal

Young kids enjoy this project. They create a notebook all about themselves—their likes and dislikes, their hopes and dreams, their world as they see it. Only this notebook is different. It's all about math, language, and self-expression.

This activity will help your children expand their perceptions of themselves. They can add to this notebook as months go by and enjoy nostalgic memories years later.

Here are some sample questions. You may wish to add or delete from this list; your children may wish to add more of their own. Your kids probably will want to have the question at the top of a page and either write their answers below or fill the rest of the page with pictures or drawings that illustrate their answers (or incorporate both).

1. What is your age in years? When were you born? What time were you born? (Baby pictures would enhance this page.)
2. What is your address? (Kids may wish to include a photograph or drawing of their home.)
3. How tall are you? How much do you weigh? (A photograph is ideal for this page.) How much have you grown since last year? Last two years?
4. List five words that describe you. (Kids may wish to look in a magazine for pictures that best illustrate these words to accompany their listing.)
5. Name five things that you most enjoy doing.
6. If you could have three wishes, what would you wish for? (Drawings or pictures would look nice on this page.) How would this make you feel?
7. Where is your favorite place to go? Why? How does it make you feel? What makes it different from other places you've been to?
8. What is your favorite Bible story? What can you learn from it to apply in your own life?

Prepare a list of questions with your children (not too many at one time, though; you don't want to overwhelm your kids). Limit activity to fifteen or twenty minutes per session. Younger kids tire easily.

If your children are too young to write, you can use a *language experience approach*. Write your children's exact responses to the questions. Let them cut out or draw their own pictures. (Younger kids may need help cutting with scissors as their fine motor skills are just developing.)

ACTIVITY 15: PERSONAL TIME LINE

Grade levels:	2 and above
Time involved:	20 to 30 minutes (will vary depending on age level)
Teacher's/parent's role:	Explain purpose and directions, provide assistance
Learning styles:	Verbal-linguistic, visual-spatial, bodily-kinesthetic, intrapersonal

Each child illustrates and writes descriptions of significant events in her life—such as an unforgettable gift, getting a new pet (or the loss of a loved pet), new brothers or sisters, travels, first day of school, first time on a bicycle, an award, and so on. The 5x7 cards are attached to yarn in chronological order. The time lines are then either vertically, horizontally, or diagonally displayed (choice is left to the child) on the walls so children can read about classmates.

This activity also can be used for children to project the events in their lives they would like to achieve or have take place.

Incidentally, be sure that you work along with your children to prepare your own time line!

OPEN SHARING

Our similarities bring us together, our differences
make us unique.

George Betts

It has been said, "no man is an island, except unto himself." In order for our society to grow in new dimensions, people must learn to work harmoniously together and challenge and help each other attain new heights. Tomorrow's visions—whether it be world peace, ending global hunger, or solving our ecological problems—only can become realities when people come together and unite hand in hand, as they pursue visions of a better tomorrow.

For this to take place, it must first begin in the home and classroom. Kids need to become aware of each other's abilities and sensitive to each other's needs. Also, kids must become aware that not only can they learn from each other, they also can grow further as they give to and receive help from each other. Cooperative learning opportunities are a must for optimal growth!

The following activities and strategies help foster positive interpersonal relationships.

ACTIVITY 16: ONE SPECIAL THING

Grade levels:	PreK and above
Time involved:	10 to 15 minutes
Teacher's/parent's role:	Guide the activity
Learning styles:	Verbal-linguistic, interpersonal

Divide your children into pairs. To the partner, a child tells as much as possible about himself. The two then switch rolls. The second child tells the first all about herself. After five minutes, the group comes together in a circle, and children introduce their partners to the group by name and share one thing that impressed them as *most special* about their partners.

Then invite your children to discuss what it was like to share information about themselves with another person and elaborate on their feelings as they heard their partners share what most impressed them.

Kids always enjoy having positive comments about themselves shared with the rest of the group. As turns are taken, "I want to be recognized, too!" is written on the face of each child.

ACTIVITY 17: CONTOUR DRAWING WITH ADJECTIVE WARDROBE

Grade levels:	1 and above
Time involved:	10 to 15 minutes
Organizational pattern:	Children are paired and face each other
Teacher's/parent's role:	Briefly provide directions and purpose of activity
Materials needed:	Paper, charcoal, pastel, marker or pencil, pen (optional)
Learning styles:	Verbal-linguistic, visual-spatial, interpersonal

Each child draws a number from a container. Kids with matching numbers pair off and become each other's subjects.

Paired children simultaneously draw a contour (or outline) drawing of the other's face. Eyes remain fixed on the partner, instead of the paper. Each artist draws slowly and carefully—sensitive to every detail (eyes, nose, hair . . .)—noting special features of the subject. When the drawing is completed, each artist then looks at her drawing and adds a list of complimentary adjectives (or positive descriptors) beneath or around the drawing.

The finished drawings can be displayed on a bulletin board, home classroom or bedroom wall, or door.

Extender: Each child may also do a self-portrait while looking into a mirror and list his or her positive attributes.

ACTIVITY 18: JOURNAL REFLECTIONS

Grade levels: 2 and above
Time involved: 10 to 15 minutes
Teacher's/parent's role: Provide purpose and direction
Materials needed: Journal, pencil or pen
Learning styles: Verbal-linguistic, musical-rhythmic, intrapersonal, interpersonal

Play soft background music and invite children to write about a particular topic. Here are several examples:

If you awakened one morning and suddenly discovered that you had turned into an animal, such as a cuddly kitten or playful puppy, which animal would you wish to be? Why? Describe your feelings.

What is the most meaningful gift that you have given someone else? To whom did you give it? How did it make the other person feel? How did it make you feel? Or: What was the most meaningful gift that you have received? Who gave it to you? How did it make you feel?

If you could have lunch with anyone in the world for one hour, with whom would you have lunch? Why? Where would you wish to have lunch? What questions would you wish to ask that person? What might be his or her responses to your questions?

Which children's story is your favorite? Why? How can you apply it to your own life? Or: Who is your favorite character in the story? Why? In what ways are you like that person? What did that person have that you would like to see developed in your own life? (The same approach can be used with Bible stories.)

When finished writing, either exchange journals with a partner or teams of three or four children, or read your reflections to each other. Provide an opportunity for each child to discuss how he felt when he wrote his feelings. Be sure you share your feelings as well.

Another approach is to exchange journal reflections and write reflective, positive comments in the journals. You will discover something: The importance you place on each child's efforts is generally the same as what each child places on yourself.

Kids always eagerly await the sharing of their reflections and to read your comments and reflections. This weekly form of written and spoken dialogue provides kids an opportunity to openly express thoughts they otherwise may be reluctant to verbalize.

Be sure that you keep a folder of each child's, as well as your own, reflection papers (if a journal isn't used). These will be fun to read and share a year from now.

ACTIVITY 19: CAR WASH

Grade levels:	PreK and above
Time involved:	5 minutes
Teacher's/parent's role:	Involve all children
Learning styles:	Verbal-linguistic, bodily-kinesthetic, interpersonal

Form two parallel lines with your children. Kids face the one directly across from them in the other line. The two lines of children become the *car wash.*

Select one child to walk slowly through the car wash. As the child passes through, car washers in both lines gently pat the child passing through on the back, while giving compliments and positive strokes.

Generally, two car washes per day are scheduled. Kids love this activity and cannot wait until it's their turn!

ACTIVITY 20: SOMETHING I'M GOOD AT

Grade levels:	4 and above
Time involved:	5 to 15 minutes (varies, depending upon size and age level of group)

Teacher's/parent's role: Involve all children
Learning styles: Verbal-linguistic, intrapersonal, interpersonal

As the family or classroom sits in a circle, each child talks about special abilities that he or she has, or ones in which he or she excels. The family or class soon discovers there is a variety, as well as an overlap, of interests and talents among its members.

At the conclusion of the individual sharing phase, a family or classroom discussion follows for elaboration on individual (and overlapping) interests, talents, or strengths that everyone has.

ACTIVITY 21: V.I.P. INTERVIEWS

Grade levels: 6 and above
Time involved: 10 to 15 minutes
Teacher's/parent's role: Ensure positive highlighting, provide questions and timing as needed
Learning styles: Verbal-linguistic, interpersonal

Two or three children each day (at the start of the year) "meet the press." One child at a time is interviewed by the other kids or homeschool teacher for five minutes, after which you provide positive highlights of that child. The two or three individual interviews can be spaced over the day to ensure the *specialness* of each child.

Alternative (for larger classes): If you feel that some children may be hesitant about personally responding to questions before a large class, you may wish to conduct this activity in a small group setting. Divide the class into groups of two or three. Each child is interviewed by her group. Following the interview, the group either shares interesting and positive highlights of the interviewed children in front of the entire group, or the group may develop a bulletin board featuring their group's V.I.P. This approach to the V.I.P. interview is done on a weekly basis until all children have been interviewed.

4

KEY 3: PEACE—RELAXING THE LEARNING ENVIRONMENT

... be still and know that I am God.

Psalm 46:10

She is waiting for her children to return from an active game following lunch. It is windy outside and hot. She dims the classroom lights. This seems to cool the room and calm the children as they come into the room.

She asks her children to find a comfortable spot on the carpet near her and begins reading from *Jessie Came Across The Sea*. After she finishes the reading, she talks about the story with her children and invites them to relate their own insights and reflections of the story. The theme for the past two weeks has been "Giving." (Yesterday, she had read *The Giving Tree*, a day earlier, *The Selfish Giant*. Last week she had read *Charlotte's Web* each day after lunch. Her children had thoroughly enjoyed those stories and the values for life that they taught, as well as the unwinding time that was provided.)

Through these sessions, she nurtures her children's love of literature and provides time to relax. The children need this time to switch gears from the high-energy noon play to the quieter focus of the early afternoon, and settling kids is much easier for her using these after-lunch readings.

DAISIES 'N DRAGONFLIES

Have you ever taken the time to carefully watch daisies and dragonflies? Regardless of the weather—how windy or rainy it is—daisies never become frightened or run and hide; they simply remain calm in the midst of a storm. And as for dragonflies: they remain unruffled and silently dance and dart throughout the sky, regardless of what is beneath or above them. We can learn much from daisies and dragonflies by quieting ourselves and the learning environment.

Kids can be anything but calm at times. They can be engaged in play or a fun activity, which is a healthy release of energy; or they can be anxious, possibly about an upcoming test, complicated learning assignment, or sibling (or peer) conflict, which only increases negative energy and tension. Such negative energy and tension serves only to prevent effective learning. Research studies continue to show that a relaxed learning environment optimizes learning, and calming strategies and activities should be incorporated into the daily curriculum.

RELAXING THE LEARNING ENVIRONMENT

A peaceful classroom, in many ways, is like a forest: There is a vibration of aliveness and quietness, with a sustaining balance. Kids *need* an atmosphere that is calm, harmonious, and nurturing. And the stage for this peace is set by the teacher, the approach, and the learning activity.

Three considerations are needed to relax the classroom. One is the physical environment.

Picture a classroom with soft lighting, color tones that are warm and stimulating, brightly colored bulletin boards, comfortable furniture, decorative plants, soft music, and learning centers that invite curiosity and participation. Such a classroom carries with it a relaxed atmosphere that encourages children's involvement and invites movement throughout the room. Kids learn best in a comfortable and attractive environment. (Think of the energy that goes into planning creature comforts in the home for ourselves. We should invest as much in designing our classrooms!)

Coupled with the physical arrangement of a classroom is the instructional approach of the teacher. It's a wise teacher who *responds* and doesn't *react,* knows when to use a calm voice, incorporates needed times of movement and relaxation, provides soft classical or inspirational music, and effectively uses quiet instructional activities to calm and release children's tension and provide a better focus for learning.

There are too many kids whose learning is minimized due to conflict, stress, and tension within the classroom. Relaxing the classroom itself does not bring about a calm learning environment, but it helps. I and many teachers and parents have found that when the learning environment is peaceful, kids will be calmer and better focused for learning.

Finally, there is a third ingredient that we need to incorporate: prayer. It is through our continued prayer to the Lord that His peace is maintained. In addition, teachers and parents need to pray for each child, as well as the school day itself. Daily prayer and meditation promote harmony and peace in the classroom and individual lives. Scripture directs this. Experience proves it.

Activities and strategies that follow are a small sampling of the unlimited possibilities that exist for promoting a peaceful learning environment.

STRATEGIES AND ACTIVITIES

Teach me so that I may learn, love me so that I may grow.

Seven-year-old child

Sometimes kids can become wound up, especially on a windy or rainy day, or sitting for extended periods of time. Tension builds and a release is needed. The activities that follow are effective with helping kids enjoy a relaxed learning environment. (As relaxation techniques have been found to be effective in natural childbirthing, the same principle can be applied to children's learning.)

ACTIVITY 22: STRETCHING ACTIVITY

Grade levels: All
Time involved: 3 to 5 minutes
Teacher's/parent's role: Model the technique
Learning styles: Bodily-kinesthetic

While standing, inhale deeply and exhale slowly, several times.
    Loosen your shoulders, neck, and arms by flexing, then completely relaxing these muscles by making them go limp.

Stretch up toward the ceiling—slowly reach as high as you can with both arms.

Repeat steps 2 and 3.

Bend at the waist and slowly reach for the floor without straining.

Relax your entire body by gently shaking it loose.

Repeat the last two steps.

Inhale deeply several times; exhale slowly. Feel your body relax as you exhale.

Now sit and relax.

ACTIVITY 23: A PEACEFUL SETTING

Sit in a comfortable position. Begin with your toes and proceed upward. Flex each muscle individually, hold it, then relax it. Continue upward until you relax your neck and your face.

Close your eyes and take several deep breaths—exhale slowly. Completely relax your body. With your eyes closed, picture a quiet place—a favorite place—on a mountaintop, beside a lake, in a grassy field, or even at home.

Imagine everything peaceful that surrounds you. Tree limbs softly swaying in a gentle breeze. A deep blue, quiet sky. (pause)

As you imagine the scene, listen to the rhythmic sounds surrounding you. The song of meadowlarks or robins. Waves gently lapping at the shore. A small stream nearby. (pause)

Feel the gentle breeze. (pause)

Touch something nearby—a handful of sand, a leaf . . . a pinecone. Something of God's handiwork outside.

Feel the sun beating down on you, warming your entire body. Let yourself relax completely.

Take two deep breaths.

Slowly open your eyes, but remain very still. Take two more deep breaths.

STEPPING INTO GOD'S CREATION

In the silence, I hear a symphony.

Anonymous

There is a natural peace that is experienced as we step into a forest, meadow, or even a city park. Somehow we are removed from the activity of our daily routines when we are in quieter surroundings. As Christ found a quiet place to pray in the Garden of Gethsemane or on a hilltop overlooking the Sea of Galilee, we too can enjoy the quietness of the outdoors. We need to understand the importance of slowing ourselves down, being still, and knowing that He is God of our lives.

The following activities enable kids to enjoy learning in quieter, outdoor settings.

ACTIVITY 24: ENJOYING NATURE

Grade levels:	All
Time involved:	Can vary
Teacher's/parent's role:	Provide direction, join the activity
Learning styles:	Bodily-kinesthetic, visual-spatial, intrapersonal, interpersonal

While you're outdoors, carefully observe the brightness of colors of the sky, clouds, trees, and grass or sand, or the beauty of a sunset that God has designed. Note the crispness and clarity of the sounds of the breeze blowing through the trees or the call of a meadowlark in the field.

Think about God's perfect plan in nature as you watch a bird soar overhead, ducks glide down a slowly moving river, or squirrels playfully scampering about. Consider the mathematical perfection of the countless stars, planets, and asteroids in the night sky, and millions of molecules in a tiny drop spilling over a craggy edge into a pool below. Although mind staggering, it provides a peace and strength knowing Who holds us and all of creation to-gether.

Bask in the glory of God's creation about you.

ACTIVITY 25: QUIET PRAYER

Grade levels: All
Time involved: 7 to 12 minutes
Teacher's/parent's role: Provide guidance; share your feelings
                         with your children
Learning styles: Bodily-kinesthetic, intrapersonal, inter-
                         personal

Find a quiet spot either outside or inside the classroom, free from distractions, and quietly have your one-on-one time with the Lord.

As you pray, take time to really listen to what He speaks to your heart and allow His perfect peace to calm and sustain you. *We are His sheep and we do know His voice, as we read in John 10. Also, Isaiah 30:21 instructs us to listen to the Lord as He tells us which way to go or what to do. We must teach our children to learn to walk and be intimate with Him.*

Although I do not ascribe to the purpose underlying some conventional relaxation techniques, the following does have a scriptural basis to it when we are aware of God's love, peace, and strength and are able to share these with others.

Focus on one of the following: loving others and being loved by God; being capable and able to help others who have needs; our own strength in Christ and sharing that strength with others through our encouragement and assistance; having purpose and direction in our lives, empathy, compassion, and understanding for others that only the Holy Spirit can provide; and feelings of peace and contentment. (*We are called to love, lift up in prayer and reach out to one another, as modeled by our Lord. I have found that when children reach out to one another, the entire classroom atmosphere changes so beautifully and is so peaceful, and positive learning in the classroom takes on new heights.)*

ACTIVITY 26: FLOATING CLOUDS

Grade levels:	All
Time involved:	20 to 40 minutes
Teacher's/parent's role:	Discuss activity and descriptively share an example
Materials needed:	Sketch pad; pencil, crayons, or pastels; writing paper
Learning styles:	Visual-spatial, verbal-linguistic, intrapersonal, interpersonal

Invite your children to gather outside and find a comfortable place to sketch and write. Ask them to look at shapes in the clouds and select ones that are particularly interesting. Provide materials for them to sketch cloud shapes and write about them, either through poetry or narrative (possibly in the form of a legend or tall tale). As the wind moves across the sky, kids might add movement to their drawings or descriptions.

With younger children, couple original sketches with language experience (child-dictated, teacher-/parent-transcribed).

At the close of the activity, invite children to share sketches, poems, and stories with others.

ACTIVITY 27: COUNTING WITH NATURE

Grade levels:	PreK to 2
Time involved:	15 to 40 minutes
Materials needed:	None
Teacher's/parent's role:	Guide activity
Learning styles:	All can be incorporated

Take your children on a nature walk and enjoy a picturesque math experience.

> I wonder how many limbs we can count on that tree over there?
>
> See the butterflies? I wonder how many there are?
>
> Look at the ducks floating in the pond! Let's count them.
>
> I wonder how many steps it will take to walk to that large rock in front of us?
>
> Let's close our eyes and listen to all the sounds we hear. When I say to open our eyes, let's find out how many sounds we can name together.
>
> Wow! Look at that army of ants. Shall we try to count them?
>
> How far can you run in fifteen seconds? I'll count while you run and we'll measure the distance. Now it's my turn. You count to fifteen while I run.

You and your kids can generate a number of math possibilities that exist on a nature walk. Not only does this activity provide number reinforcement, it's also invigorating!

Activity 28: Environment Awareness

Grade levels:	All
Time involved:	Varies
Teacher's/parent's role:	Guide activity
Learning styles:	Verbal-linguistic, visual-spatial, intra-personal, interpersonal

Take your children on a nature walk. An ideal setting is a neighborhood park, mountains or forest, the ocean shore, meadow, or pond, free from man-made noise. Find something natural of interest: a boulder, plant, or tree—something that is stationary. Share with your children how each part of creation has a role in nature and the importance of preserving nature.

Invite your children to observe something in motion: Perhaps a butterfly fluttering about overhead, a flower bud about to unfold its petals to a bright new day, clouds floating across the sky, a hermit crab in search of an empty shell by the seashore, or even a piece of driftwood floating by the shore.

Two beautiful books to share are Lynn Cherry's *The Great Kapok Tree* (grades K-6) and *A River Ran Wild* (grades 3–6). Each book is beautifully illustrated and vividly shares the importance of preserving the environment. *The Great Kapok Tree* looks at the cutting down of the Amazon Rain Forest from the perspective of animals that habitat the region; *A River Ran Wild* shows what can occur when man disregards the cleanliness of the environment and ecological balance of nature.

Provide each child an opportunity to share his or her feelings.

ACTIVITY 29: GROWING FLOWER

Grade levels:	PreK-3
Time involved:	15 to 30 minutes (depending upon size of group and activities incorporated)
Teacher's/parent's role:	Provide narration, guide activity
Materials needed:	Sketch pad, watercolors, pastels, acrylics, marking pens
Learning styles:	Verbal-linguistic, visual-spatial, bodily-kinesthetic, intrapersonal, interpersonal

Try this learning activity. Have your children close their eyes as you relate the following passage to them. (Be sure to enhance this prose with descriptions added by you or your children.) During the narration, extend the activity through creative movement. Have kids pantomime the words or sentences. Or, after the reading, have them share what it must be like for a seed to become a flower, and possibly even paint or illustrate what they imagine the seed and flower may look like.

The Growing Flower

You are a seed below the dark, frozen, stiff ground. Everything around you is dry and hard; restraining and containing. You are still, silent, waiting; your heart hopes for spring. Now a soothing warmth creeps around you. Things begin to move inside. You are wakening, stirring. You stretch.

The soil is softened by rain and warmth. You shove, extend, out and up. You grow, reach, push, and nudge. And one day, something wonderful happens: You burst through the earth into sunlight. And oh! The sun is bright and gleaming, summery-warm.

But sepals bind you like a snug winter coat. The sun blazes deeper and deeper. You grow and push taller and higher. Your sepals spread apart, move back toward the stem, then shed, no longer needed.

Your glorious petals stretch up and out. You feel beautiful. Everything about you is fresh, vivid, exciting, new. A bee buzzes by and pauses to sip your nectar. A butterfly flutters past. Life sings about you. And you dance in the gentle rhythm of a soft breeze. People stop to look at you and admire your beauty and fragrance.

You smile. You are a beautiful, miracle flower of God's creation.

Now open your eyes very slowly. Remain quiet and relaxed, Beautiful Flower.

SOLITUDE

Alone with my thoughts, I can dream forever.

Anonymous

Kids often find themselves in a patchwork of events, concerns, and activities, thus failing to take some time to relax and be at peace within themselves. It is when they quietly become absorbed in the ecstasy of a setting sun, desert rain, or sounds of a forest that they are able to feel a peace in all that has been created. The same can hold true for a classroom or home: Children need to be able to enjoy a relaxed, peaceful learning environment.

Activities that follow provide opportunity for kids to enjoy a relaxed learning environment. Inner spirits are quieted. The classroom climate is calmed. A sharper focus on learning develops.

ACTIVITY 30: SOUNDS OF SILENCE

Grade levels: All
Time involved: Varies
Classroom organization: Children are seated in a circle
Teacher's/parent's role: Guide activity
Materials needed: None
Learning styles: Verbal-linguistic, intrapersonal, interpersonal

Here is a fun learning activity that is also thought provoking. Present the first question (according to age appropriateness) and invite each child briefly to respond to it or "pass." Continue in the same manner with the second question, and so forth.

1. What is the sound of happiness?
2. What color is love?
3. What are the voices of summer? Winter? Spring? Fall? (Select one season)
4. What is the sound of a falling snowflake?
5. What piece of music describes a sunrise (or a sunset)?
6. What are the smells of a desert rain?
7. What are the sounds of the forest at night?
8. What are the colors of warmth? Cold? Fear? Security? Softness? (Select one)
9. What can you see more clearly with closed eyes?
10. What is the texture of a smile? A frown? Hurt feelings? (Select one)

This can serve as an excellent springboard for descriptive writing.

ACTIVITY 31: REFLECTION PAPER

Grade levels: K-6
Time involved: Can vary
Teacher's/parent's role: Guide the activity
Materials needed: Selected cassette tape or CD and player, writing paper, pen or pencil, sketch pad, marking pens or crayons
Learning styles: Musical-rhythmic, visual-spatial, verbal-linguistic, intrapersonal

This is an excellent relaxation exercise and tension releaser. Place soft, easy listening, inspirational, or light classical music while children write their thoughts on paper. (Younger children may wish to doodle with crayons, marking pens or pencils, or write some words that express their thoughts or feelings.)

Invite children to leave the reflection papers with you and individually discuss them with each child at a later time. Or write positive responses on their papers and return them to your children either later in the day or the following day. This provides a great start for eventual journal writing.

ACTIVITY 32: WRITING TO MUSIC

Grade levels: 2 and above
Time involved: 10 to 30 minutes
Teacher's/parent's role: Model a relaxation exercise and set the stage for writing
Materials needed: Classical or inspirational CD or cassette tape (and player); writing paper and pen or pencil; art paper and pencils, pastels, watercolors, or acrylics
Learning styles: Musical-rhythmic, verbal-linguistic, visual-spatial, intrapersonal, interpersonal

An excellent way to combine relaxation, creativity, music appreciation, and language arts is to have children write to music. Selections can include "Waltz of the Flowers," from Tchaikovsky's *Nutcracker Suite*; Mozart's "The Impresario Overture;" J. Strauss' "Blue Danube;" Chopin's "Fantaisie—Impromptu in C-Sharp Minor;" Brahms' "Lullaby;" Beethoven's "Pastoral Symphony" from his *Symphony No. 6*; and "Clair de Lune" from Debussy's *Suite Bergamasque*. Soft inspirational music also is very effective, such as Mary Beth Carlson's *In This Quiet Place* or Dino's *Peace in the Midst of a Storm*.

Ask your kids to be seated comfortably. Play the selected music. Use statements such as the following to lead children through this activity.

Close your eyes and imagine the scene the music is portraying. As the music continues to play, describe your scene either in writing or illustration, using a pencil, pastels, watercolors, acrylics, or any medium you choose.

(Hint: With shorter pieces, replay the selection at this time; with longer versions, continue playing during this writing or illustrating phase.)

Also, you may wish to softly play soothing music during those times when children are quietly working on individual assignments or taking an exam. Music is a wonderful way to calm the learning environment. Further, children tend to perform better academically during such times.

ACTIVITY 33: IMAGINARY TRIP

Grade levels:	All
Time involved:	Varies
Teacher's/parent's role:	Guide activity
Learning styles:	Verbal-linguistic, visual-spatial, intrapersonal

You have just finished reading Eric Carle's *The Very Hungry Caterpillar*, and you invite your children to get comfortable and close their eyes. Staying with the theme of this book, you're going to let them imagine what it might be like to be a butterfly.

79

Imagine yourself as a butterfly that soars high in the sky, far, far away. . . . You enjoy the clean, fresh air, the clouds, and the sunlight above, and the view of the countryside below you.

You feel free and happy to be in the sky. . . . You feel light, carefree, and airy, free to fly wherever you wish. . . . You feel there is nothing you cannot do. . . . You feel as though you can dance in the air and do cartwheels, spins, and loops.

Now you decide to fly down to a daffodil. As you alight on its petals, you smell the clean fragrance. . . . You feel nicely balanced as the flower gently sways in the late morning breeze.

You look up and see a very young child with an outstretched hand slowly reaching toward you, index finger extended. You fly toward the hand and alight on the finger as the child giggles with glee.

Children share what it felt like to be a butterfly and describe butterflies they have enjoyed watching in their own backyards and neighboring parks or meadows, as well as those that have landed on their own outstretched fingers.

ACTIVITY 34: D.E.A.R. (DROP EVERYTHING AND READ)

Grade levels:	1 and above
Time involved:	Approximately 15 to 20 minutes (can vary depending upon age)
Teacher's/parent's role:	Join children in the reading activity
Learning styles:	Verbal-linguistic, intrapersonal

Select a fifteen- to twenty-minute time period each week—perhaps twice weekly (or more)—to stop all other activity and read. Reading material can be a book or appropriate magazine. The entire classroom or household is involved.

What takes place is not only a quiet, reflective period of rest, but also a demonstrated value of reading. Classrooms and homes that have practiced this have found an increase in reading enjoyment and performance.

5

KEY 4: TRUST—DEVELOPING A
TRUSTING LEARNING CLIMATE

Trust in the Lord with all your heart; and lean not unto your
own understanding. In all your ways acknowledge Him, and
He will direct your paths.

Proverbs 3:5–6

This fourth key is actually a dual need: Kids need to feel *secure* within themselves—that is, have a trust in their own abilities and potential; also, kids need to be able to have an unwavering trust in their parents, teachers, and classmates or siblings. As kids are taught to trust God in all things, they also must learn to have trust in us. And this trust must never be violated.

The greatest fear of children (and adults) is a breaking of trust. In the classroom or home, this often takes the form of humiliation or ridicule, teacher or peer rejection, or a breach of confidence. And it is in this type of environment that children no longer feel safe. Trust has been violated. And without it, learning is minimized, as well as individual growth. Safety zones are tightened and withdrawal can take place.

Now, picture a learning environment in which kids and teacher are eagerly, genuinely helping each other to grow and learn. Cooperatively learning. Giving to others. Receiving from others. Trusting one's own abilities. Having a steadfast confidence in the teacher or parent—trusting her that she is ever mindful of her children's best interests and needs. Unless a spirit of mutual trust exists within the classroom or home, individual learning and growth will be impeded.

RISKS AND LEAPS

For kids to ascend to a new level, whether it be speaking in front of others, learning a new math concept, trying a new science experiment with an unpredictable outcome, learning how to play an instrument, or how to do a folk dance, they must take a certain measure of risk. To venture that risk, kids must feel safe.

Kids, in a very real sense, must learn to become risk-takers and, at times, take quantum leaps into new areas. This prepares them for later life expansion as they investigate new ideas, delve into new areas, and take on new roles. Studies indicate that kids who perceive themselves as being "safe" are more comfortable when taking a risk; those who are less secure tend to avoid risk-taking situations.

CLASSROOM APPLICATIONS

In the classroom, among young children, it may simply be a matter of "taking turns" and sharing. In cooperative learning, trust certainly must be present; otherwise, cooperative learning would quickly change to competitive learning or withdrawal altogether. For a child to ask another for help with regrouping involving three-digit subtraction where zeros are involved implies admission of a need for help, trusting that the child's "need" won't be broadcasted to his or her detriment. On occasions, I've seen classroom teachers, as well as parents, humiliate children before others. Generally, the humiliation is unintentional; nevertheless, trust has been violated. Emotional safety has been taken away. And the child's self-image begins to crack.

Strategies and activities that follow provide sample approaches that will foster a trusting environment where kids, teachers and parents are nurturers, encouragers, and supporters of each other.

Strategies and Activities

The great man is he who does not lose his child's heart.

Mencius

Activity 35: Trust Walk

Grade levels:	All
Time involved:	15 to 30 minutes
Teacher's/parent's role:	Provide guidance, carefully supervise
Learning styles:	Bodily-kinesthetic, verbal-linguistic, intrapersonal, interpersonal

Team kids into pairs: One is blindfolded, the other is not and serves as a guide. The sighted partner will gently hold the upper arm of her blindfolded partner and guide him throughout a building or outdoors area. (Be sure to keep all pairs of children in one large group so that you are able to carefully monitor the activity.)

Each guide will invite her partner to use senses of hearing and touch to investigate the environment. As guides escort their partners through a world without sight, blindfolded members come to a deeper realization of what life would be like without sight and the importance of the senses of hearing and touch.

After ten or fifteen minutes, partners are asked to reverse roles. When the activity is finished, sit down with your kids and discuss the following: *What did it feel like to be blind? How much did you rely on your other senses? What did your partner do that built your trust in her? For those who are blindfolded first, did you feel a greater sense of responsibility when you became the guide (than what you may have had if you had not been previously blindfolded)?*

ACTIVITY 36: BEING A FRIEND

Grade levels:	All
Time involved:	Varies
Teacher's/parent's role:	Provide responsive communication in an informal atmosphere
Learning styles:	Verbal-linguistic, interpersonal

We should join children for non-academic activities. Kids deeply appreciate a teacher who takes time in between and around instructional time to be with them. Whether it's participating in a game, an outdoor picnic lunch, or small group conversation, the specific activity may be incidental, *but the relationship is vital.* Some of the most productive moments as teachers or parents take place in such informal settings. Children need a teacher or parent who is also a guide, counselor, coach, tutor, and the host of remaining roles incumbent upon caring and involvement.

ACTIVITY 37: PERSONAL SHARING

Grade levels:	All
Time involved:	Varies
Teacher's/parent's role:	Provide responsive communication in an informal atmosphere
Learning styles:	Verbal-linguistic, interpersonal

I have found this to be the most effective way to develop interpersonal trust. When kids can learn to share openly with one another, a deeper closeness develops with one another and class-room or family unity.

There are several ways to designate partners: selection by the kids, teacher or parent, or names drawn from a container. All three can be used interchangeably. (If there is an odd number of kids, then the classroom teacher or parent partners with one.)

It is recommended that partners be changed periodically.

ACTIVITY 38: TEMPERATURE READINGS

Grade levels:	PreK and above
Time involved:	A few minutes
Teacher's/parent's role:	Provide an opportunity for each child to respond; provide positive feedback
Learning styles:	Verbal-linguistic, intrapersonal, interpersonal

Ask children to share their emotional temperature reading for the day (scale of 1 to 10, 10 as high).

10 – Extremely happy—doing cartwheels!
9 – Very happy—everything's going great!
8 – Quite happy—good day so far!
7 – Happy—things are pretty good.
6 – Somewhat happy.
5 – So-so—not bad, not great.
4 – Less than so-so—could be better.
3 – Lots less than so-so—not so hot.
2 – Unhappy—not a good day today.
1 – Bad day—need lots of TLC.

Temperature readings can be done daily at the start of the morning. This develops empathy and awareness among your children and sensitivity to one another.

ACTIVITY 39: GRAFFITI BOARD

Grade levels: K and above
Organizational pattern: Set aside a bulletin board (changed weekly)
Teacher's/parent's role: Provide purpose and direction; include only positive comments and drawings
Materials needed: Paper-covered mounted bulletin board, marking pens
Learning styles: Verbal-linguistic, visual-spatial, interpersonal

Designate a bulletin board as a classroom "graffiti board" and let your children make constructive, positive comments or drawings on butcher paper (attached to the bulletin board). Use this in conjunction with the Person of the Week (page 87) or for the entire class or family. Be certain to replace the graffiti paper each week.

ACTIVITY 40: WHAT'S YOUR SUGGESTION?

Grade levels: All
Time involved: Varies
Teacher's/parent's role: Explain the purpose and procedure of the activity
Learning areas: Communication, sharing of ideas
Materials needed: Suggestion box

Leave a suggestion box in the classroom and invite your children to write suggestions for classroom arrangements, field trips, topics for discussion, or sharing a concern. You can think of many other uses!

Some children are reticent about openly sharing in a larger group, and a suggestion box provides a discrete way for them to contribute their ideas.

ACTIVITY 41: PERSON OF THE WEEK

Grade levels: PreK and above
Teacher's/parent's role: Provide purpose, direction, and assistance
Learning styles: Verbal-linguistic, visual-spatial, interpersonal

A child is randomly selected as "Person of the Week," and a positive bulletin board is developed by the others expressly for this child. Classmates and teacher (or parent and siblings) search magazines for appropriate pictures, develop artwork, design an adjective wardrobe (see page 61), and so on, to highlight the featured child. Each person expresses through pictures or words admirable qualities of the person of the week.

ACTIVITY 42: READ ALL ABOUT US!

Grade levels: K and above
Time involved: Varies
Teacher's/parent's role: Ensure that each child contributes in one way or another
Materials needed: Plain white paper, word processor or typewriter, marking pens
Learning styles: Verbal-linguistic, mathematical-logical, visual-spatial, intrapersonal, interpersonal

Have your children help create a group newspaper or newsletter: Each child contributes stories and poems she and other children have written, interesting class activities, individual accomplishments, and upcoming events or trips. This is an effective way for your kids to see their names and efforts in print!

Children help determine the newspaper layout and graphics; older kids can be in charge of the overall production. Your kids can help type or keyboard the stories and articles onto sheets to be copied.

Class newspapers help kids with writing and communication skills, art, typing/keyboarding, and individual creativity. Young children enjoy dictating stores and poems for their teacher or parent to put into print.

Incidentally, be sure to keep a collection of classroom newspapers or newsletter issues and have them bound for later nostalgia.

CONTINUING BRIDGES

Blessed is the teacher who answers simply the startling questions, for she shall always be trusted.

Old proverb

Kids cannot remain islands to themselves. They must build bridges to each other. The richer the network in terms of quality relationships, the greater the foundation for each child upon which to build, for it is on this foundation that children learn to encourage and support one another.

As this is what we are to do for each other, so is this to take place in the classroom or home. In so doing, children will have the emotional and academic support to scale to even greater heights. And all this stems from two things: One, a willingness in children to help and support one another; and two, an existence of mutual trust.

Activities and strategies that follow are focused on developing such a network of mutual trust in specific academic content areas (yet they are not restricted exclusively to those subject areas).

ACTIVITY 43: BUDDY SYSTEM

Grade levels: K and above
Teacher's/parent's role: Provide guidance, assist when needed
Learning styles: Interpersonal and any combination of the
                          others

One school finds a buddy system useful with math and spelling, as well as other subject areas. They find that sometimes peers can explain a particular math algorithm or science concept more effectively at times than their teacher. (It's a humbling, yet realistic experience.) This, they feel, helps to cement each child's understanding of social studies or math concepts, as well as reinforces positive interpersonal relationships.

Their teacher has also found that each child's academic performance has climbed dramatically, as each buddy session becomes an applied experience.

ACTIVITY 44: CROSS-AGE TUTORING

Grade levels:	All
Time involved:	Varies
Organizational pattern:	Older kids paired with younger children
Teacher's/parent's role:	Provide tutorial instruction to older kids; assist where needed
Learning styles:	Interpersonal and any combination of the others

In a small central California school district, the school principal conducts a school-wide, cross-age tutoring reading program for forty minutes twice a week at the elementary school. Grade levels are paired as follows: grades K-1 and 4, 2 and 5, and 3 and 6. Upper grade children listen (and read) to lower grade children and assist younger children with oral reading and decoding skills. (Identified upper grade remedial readers make significant strides while involved in the cross-age reading program.)

Clearly, the tutorial program reinforces the skills of *both* groups of kids. Both groups enjoy being involved in the program and the benefits grained from it. This approach has been used by a number of classrooms and large homeschool groups with successful outcomes.

ACTIVITY 45: SPELLING GROUPS

Grade levels:	2 and above
Content areas:	Can be applied to all subject areas
Teacher's/parent's role:	Explain the small group process, provide an example of a week's group study plan
Learning styles:	Interpersonal and any combination of the others

A classroom teacher has her children self-direct their learning under careful guidance. The children are pretested at the start of the school year and given appropriate word lists for their respective grade levels. The kids, in small ability level groups of three or four children, select words to study from their group's list. Each group selects a weekly group leader who, with input from the group, maps the week's study plan for the group.

The following is a sample plan:

Monday: Select twenty words and individually develop a crossword puzzle for another group member to solve the following day. Study ten of the words (this is worked on at school and at home), using an appropriate learning styles approach presented in chapter 3.

Tuesday: In a buddy system, two children test each other on the ten words. For every word that is misspelled, they prepare with a brief, intense study (using their individual learning styles approach) for an immediate retest. Kids then use the ten words in a drawing. The outline of whatever is being drawn consists of each of the ten words written three times. (Many kids detest writing each word ten or twenty times in what is typically assigned in many classrooms, but they enjoy creating a picture with their words, and are more cautious about spelling each word correctly. The interesting thing about this is that kids enjoy practicing words they once resented.)

Wednesday: In a buddy system, two children test each other on the next set of ten words. This time, they feed words into a software program which generates one of a variety of spelling exercises or activities for them. (Teachers or parents who do not have a spelling software package may incorporate any one of a number of spelling reinforcement activities. One such approach is for kids to use any ten or more of their words in lyrics they create to a well-known tune.)

Thursday: Children return to partners for testing on all twenty words. Groups then select a spelling game to review their words. (It's interesting to note that motivating activities tend to encourage involvement and, ultimately, foster faster spelling growth.)

Friday: The group leader will then test the group on the twenty words, score them privately, give the scored papers to their teacher (for review), who enters children's grades in the grade book and returns scored tests to the children. (A member within each group leader's group gives the group leader the spelling test, scores it privately, then submits it to the teacher.) A new group leader is selected for the following week. This way, each child has an opportunity to serve in a leadership role.

The test is not monitored by the teacher, who added that she had not experienced an episode of cheating during the past five years of using this approach. Her children experience success *and* much faster growth. (As with most classrooms, some of her children are functioning at a lower grade level in spelling, while others are much higher. With this approach, children are met at their respective levels.)

ACTIVITY 46: NOTATION/PAIRED DISCUSSION

Grade levels:	3 and above
Content areas:	Any area that involves expository reading
Time involved:	Will vary, but generally 20 minutes
Organizational pattern:	Group kids in pairs
Teacher's/parent's role:	Describe and model notation and paired discussion, guide activity
Learning styles:	Verbal-linguistic, intrapersonal, interpersonal

Have kids silently read the passage of a text and lightly write a check ✔ with a pencil beside everything they already know, a + by everything that is new, and an ! by anything that captures their attention. (A variation is to use "stick-em notes" and place them onto the page.)

When finished with notation, each child is to join a partner and discuss things found in the passage that were new, already known, and interesting. About five minutes will be needed for their discussion.

Next, have each child briefly share with the class what was interesting or new. Share your findings, too.

(Notation/paired discussion is a very effective way to get kids involved in reading. However, this should not be used as a daily regimen, nor as the primary focus in the text. This strategy is best used with a pre-selected portion of the text—not to exceed a page, unless a highly interesting section is being read by older children.)

ACTIVITY 47: PAIRED READING

Grade levels:	2 and above
Content areas:	Any content reading area
Time involved:	15 to 30 minutes (varies with age and reading level)
Teacher's/parent's role:	Describe and guide activity
Learning styles:	Verbal-linguistic, intrapersonal, interpersonal

Have kids read a short passage in a text or newspaper/magazine article), and notate (see preceding activity).

Group children in pairs. One becomes the listener, the other the recaller. The recaller relates from memory what was read in the passage; the listener waits for the recaller to finish, then she adds whatever additional information she recalls. Roles are switched several times as both children together try to reconstruct the passage read.

Whatever is forgotten by both children, or questions that may arise in terms of accuracy of their retelling, can easily be corrected by a quick check with the text passage.

Children then discuss the points they found to be most interesting, in pairs and with the entire class.

ACTIVITY 48: PAIRED QUESTIONING

Grade levels:	2 and above
Content areas:	Any content reading area
Time involved:	15 to 30 minutes
Teacher's/parent's role:	Describe and guide activity
Learning styles:	Verbal-linguistic, intrapersonal, interpersonal

Have children read a short passage in a text or newspaper/magazine article, and notate.

Group children in pairs: One becomes the questioner, the other the recaller. The questioner asks questions about the passage read; the recaller tries to recall what was read.

Next, the two children reverse roles of questioner and recaller, and reconstruct together the passage read.

Children may refer to the passage read once they have exhausted their short-term memory recall and wish to check their answers for accuracy.

Kids then discuss the points they found to be most interesting, in pairs and with the entire class.

ACTIVITY 49: JIGSAW APPROACH

Grade levels:	3 and above
Content area:	Any content reading area
Time involved:	15 to 30 minutes
Teacher's/parent's role:	Describe and guide activity
Learning styles:	Verbal-linguistic, intrapersonal, interpersonal

The *jigsaw approach* is a variation that I have found to be effective. Children are divided into groups of three or four. Each child is given a "piece" of a selected passage to read and share with the rest of the group. This form of cooperative learning is wonderful and children learn to help one another with content learning and understanding.

ACTIVITY 50: PARTNER JOURNALS

Grade levels: 2 and up
Time involved: 5 to 10 minutes
Teacher's/parent's role: Provide explanation, guide activity
Learning styles: Verbal-linguistic, intrapersonal, interpersonal

Pair your children. Each is to write reflections in his journal to his partner. Partners then exchange journals and write a responsive reflection beneath their partner's reflection.

This can be done in literature (for example, reflecting on a story scene or event both are reading), math (sharing a project idea on *probability* or *geometry*), social studies (reflecting on Patrick Henry's courage during the American Revolution), or science (the plight of dolphins), to cite several examples. For younger children, it can be their feelings about Wilbur's fear, Charlotte's compassion, or Templeton's selfishness in *Charlotte's Web*, or a particular "story" that they are writing, or whatever.

Partner journals help develop a trusting relationship among kids and provide for an enjoyable exchange of ideas!

6

KEY 5: JOY—MOTIVATING KIDS' LEARNING

. . . in your presence is fullness of joy.

Psalm 16:11

Young children, before entering formal school (conventional classroom or homeschool), acquire knowledge and an understanding of the world around them by direct experiences within their environment: They taste, smell, touch, see, hear . . . and they understand. Yet, oftentimes when a child begins formal education, much of what the child experiences lacks the interaction that she was so accustomed to. Percents or fractions in math, concepts in social studies (e.g., *division of labor* or *bigotry*), and natural forces such as gravity and pressure are reduced to terms committed to memory, not constructs experienced. True-to-life learning and children's interests take a secondary or sometimes nonexistent role.

"Why do we have to study this?"

"How am I gonna use this positive and negative integer stuff in real life?"

All too often the textbook is considered the sole source of learning, and for kids learning is lifeless. The daily routine in such classes varies little.

"Children, I would like for you to read pages 97 to 108 in your science textbook and answer the questions at the end of the chapter. Be sure to write the entire question and answer it in complete sentences. And I want every child to list the twenty-five bold-faced vocabulary words from the chapter in their textbook, copy their definitions from the glossary at the back of your text, and memorize vocabulary words and their definitions for a test this Friday."

This is busywork with little relevance to true learning. No wonder so many kids lose interest in formal learning. Lacking are true learning experiences to which kids can relate the concepts and skills that are presented. We know that in order for a child to learn to read, the child must be able to recognize the words that are to be read. And in order for a child to understand the meaning of those words, the child must be able to relate those words to previous experiences.

This principle applies to anything that is learned. Kids should be drawn into the learning process through curriculum content that uses meaningful learning experiences. To do this we need to present a realistic and relevant curriculum to kids, and show them how classroom learning relates to their lives outside of their classroom. Involving kids in such relevant, motivating learning experiences provides a deeper understanding of concepts and development of skills, as well as enjoyment of the learning experience, which will have long-lasting effects.

WHAT RESEARCH SHOWS

Research studies continue to reveal that kids learn best when they have enjoyment both in learning and in life. When there is an inner calm and motivation in learning, biochemicals from the limbic system (midbrain) flow more easily, thereby creating uninhibited learning, enabling a greater flow of neural enhancers that provide a sustained peace and focus, allow for quicker, richer dendritical growth as learning is patterned within the brain, and releases an exuberance for learning. This type of positive cycle feeds so beautifully on itself: Kids who are content and relaxed within themselves feel safe in their environment, and have success and enjoyment in what they're learning. They will grasp concepts more easily, retain what they've learned more effectively, and become more successful learners in the process. And the sky's the limit for them.

The section that follows provides a montage of activities within specific subject areas, as well as across the curriculum, each of which becomes a motivating (or joyful) learning experience for children.

STRATEGIES AND ACTIVITIES

In order to kindle others, we ourselves must glow.

Old Arabian proverb

ACTIVITY 51: TELL ME A STORY

Grade levels:	All
Time involved:	Varies (generally 10 to 30 minutes)
Teacher's/parent's role:	Read a good *bedtime* story to your child(ren)
Materials needed:	A good children's book, plus whatever materials that are needed for any additional learning activity
Learning styles:	Verbal-linguistic, interpersonal, visual-spatial (as well as others, depending upon the learning activity added)

I don't know of anyone who does not like being read to. Young children love to climb onto a parent's lap, or lie in bed with a parent seated bedside, and be taken to lands far away in distance or time. An evening regimen of reading aloud to your child provides a time of special bonding, as well as a deepened appreciation for literature.

Scheherazade (*1001 Arabian Nights*) certainly utilized an effective approach: Read a small book or portion of a longer book (or tell a story) each night and leave the appetite whetted for more. Kids eagerly look forward to each evening's story (or in the classroom, each afternoon's story). My son, Jared, enjoyed bedtime stories when he was young. And we would oftentimes read the story to each other.

Discuss the story with your child, and invite your child to close her eyes and envision herself as the heroine in a story. Ask her about her adventures, and encourage her to visually describe characters and scenes in her imagined story.

Your child may wish to make puppets (*The Three Little Pigs, Snow White and the Seven Dwarfs*, etc.) and dramatize a selected scene or the entire story.

Beautifully illustrated books for bedtime reading:

Aardema, Verna	*Why Mosquitos Buzz in People's Ears*
Aruego, Jose	*We Hide, You Seek*
Asch, Frank	*Happy Birthday, Moon*
	Moon Shadow
	Mooncake
Baker, Olaf	*Where the Buffaloes Begin*
Brown, Marcia	*Cinderella*
Carle, Eric	*Brown Bear, Brown Bear, What Do You See?*
	The Honeybee and the Robber
	The Very Busy Spider
	The Very Quiet Cricket
	The Very Hungry Caterpillar
	The Rooster Who Went Around the World
	Papa, Please Get the Moon for Me
de Paola, Tomie	*The Friendly Beasts: An Old English Christmas Carol*
	The Night Before Christmas

Drescher, Henrik	*Whose Furry Nose? Australian Animals You'd Like to Meet*
Ehlert, Lois	*Planting a Rainbow*
Forest, Heather	*A Big Quiet House: A Yiddish Folk Tale*
Flourny, Valerie	*Patchwork Quilt*
Frasconi, Antonio	*The Elephant and His Secret*
	The Snow and the Sun
	The House that Jack Built
Gantschev, Ivan	*The Train to Grandma's*
Goble, Paul	*The Girl Who Loved Wild Horses*
Graham, Gail B.	*The Beggar in the Blanket and Other Vietnamese Tales*
Hall, Donald	*Ox-Cart Man*
Halse, Gillian	*Morris, Where Are You?*
Keats, Ezra Jack	*The Snowy Day*
Kellogg, Steven	*Pecos Bill*
Lobel, Arnold	*Grasshopper on the Road*
	Frog and Toad are Friends
	Frog and Toad Together
McCloskey, Robert	*Blueberries for Sally*
	One Morning in Maine
Oakley, Robert	*The Church Mice Adrift*
Plourde, Lynn	*Pigs in the Mud in the Middle of the Rud*
Rey, Hans	*Curious George*
Rosen, Michael J.	*The Dog Who Walked with God*
Seuss, Dr.	*The Cat in the Hat*
	Green Eggs and Ham
	And to Think I Saw it on Mulberry Street
Spier, Peter	*Noah's Ark*
	The Fox Went Out on a Chilly Night
	The Pet Store
	The Toy Shop
Steig, William	*Sylvester and the Magic Pebble*
Trafuri, Nancy	*Spots, Feathers and Curly Tails*
Tudor, Tasha	*A Book of Christmas*
Waddell, Martin	*Mimi and the Dream House*
	Mimi and the Picnic

Wilde, Oscar	*The Selfish Giant*
Yin	*The Silk Thread*
Zemach, Margot	*It Could Always Be Worse*

ACTIVITY 52: ROUND-ROBIN WRITING

Grade levels:	3 and above
Time involved:	30 to 40 minutes
Organization pattern:	A whole class circle or groups of four to six kids
Teacher's/parent's role:	Provide purpose and direction, monitor time (optional: join the activity!)
Learning styles:	Verbal-linguistic, visual-spatial, musical-rhythmic, intrapersonal, interpersonal

Kids randomly select a number from a box. The child with the lowest number goes to the bulletin board (or marker board) and selects one of a number of interesting magazine pictures taped to the board or wall; child number two follows; and so on.

(Variation: Dispense with the numbers. Instead, begin circulating pictures clockwise and counterclockwise simultaneously. Kids select picture of choice as pictures are passed around the circle.)

Seated in a circle, each child staples or paperclips the picture into several sheets of lined notebook paper. Inform kids they will have about three minutes to write about their pictures. (They may start their stories at the beginning, middle, or end!) When time is called, each child passes her picture to the person at her right. Extra time is given for kids to read the previous child's entry and continue writing the story. As each "round" continues, the time is increased correspondingly to allow time for reading. At the end of the time limit, children again pass their stories to the right. This process continues for anywhere from four to seven rounds, depending upon the age factor and time element. After the final round, the stories are passed clockwise (in the opposite direction) to the original owner.

Kids then form groups of four, five, or six and share their stories with their group. Each group selects its most interesting or humorous story and shares it with the others.

Kids then break into pairs, make necessary grammatical and mechanical corrections on their own stories, and provide illustrations. The stories from all the children are then displayed throughout the classroom or home.

ACTIVITY 53: WRITERS' WORKSHOP

Grade levels: All
Teacher's/parent's role: Provide relevant learning experiences in
                          the language arts
Learning styles: All can be incorporated

While teaching middle school language arts, one teacher questioned the practice of teaching grammar, as well as punctuation, by the rules, covering one to two pages of text per class session, and taking a test at the end of the week over the material studied. Even though there were often a number of kids who scored well on the test, in a composition these same kids continued to commit the same patterns of errors taught the previous week. (In fact, research shows that teaching grammar by diagramming produces good diagrammers, not necessarily good writers. The same principle holds true for teaching grammar and punctuation "by the rules.")

The teacher began incorporating a writers' workshop in his language arts class and *involving* kids in a meaningful and relevant daily writing experience. Kids would work individually or collectively on a particular writing project, then break into small groups and constructively critique each other's writings. Soon they began to realize they weren't writing for the teacher, but actually a readership of peers. He soon noted changes in both kids' attitudes and writing growth. His kids eventually were creating fiction, poetry, editorials, position papers, dramatic plays, and "research" papers, and were *developing into writers* in the true sense. Classroom artists provided illustrations for "books" and short stories, as well as displays and set designs for play productions. The teacher worked with kids either one-on-one or in small groups (as the need arose) on specific writing skills.

As the writers' workshop continued for the remaining seven months of the school year, the teacher found his kids were writing better, *understanding* what they were learning, and thoroughly enjoying it. They were even "publishing" their works in class and school newspapers, anthologies, community newspapers, and even young writers' magazines. The key factor was *involving* kids—actively engaging them in learning experiences.

(And as for the yearly standardized achievement test? They outscored every other class in the grammar and writing mechanics sections!)

A number of classroom teachers have utilized this same approach and found similar outcomes.

ACTIVITY 54: EVENING OF THE EMINENTS

Grade levels:	3 and above
Time involved:	Varies (allow ample time for research and preparation)
Teacher's/parent's role:	Discuss several eminents beforehand with your class or family; provide materials, resources, and assistance with children's research
Learning styles:	All are incorporated

Invite kids to list several eminents (famous people, past or present, including Bible personalities) whom they admire and let each child select a favorite eminent to research and represent before parents or community. Kids become experts on their eminents through individual research. (Ample time for research and access to the school library/media center are provided.)

Kids are encouraged to become the person—in dress, mannerisms, dialect (if applicable)—and familiarize themselves with their eminent's accomplishments and background. (Note: Secondary level kids, of course, will have a more sophisticated presentation in comparison to what has been described and probably will prefer to go into greater detail.)

The evening presentation begins with eminents (without divulging their identities) mingling with guests. Parents and other family or community members as "guests" converse with eminents and privately attempt to identify each one.

Following the discovering of identities, a buffet or international dinner is held. (Each family brings a dish that represents the son or daughter's character's culture.) This provides a superb and enjoyable learning experience for all participants (eminents and guests) and helps to provide a bonding between parents and the school. (Provision for media coverage of the event can be made as well—local TV station or newspaper, as well as classroom camcorder.)

ACTIVITY 55: KID-PLANNED UNITS

Grade levels:	PreK and above
Teacher's/parent's role:	Elicit children's ideas, involve all children
Learning styles:	All are accommodated

The following is my observation of a creative student teacher whom I supervised while she was presenting a lesson to her second-graders.

The student teacher had asked the class what they would like to study in their unit on an African rainforest.

Louie:	*"Can we draw and paint a river?"*
Shannon:	*"Can we make some real trees in our classroom?"*
Brett:	*"Let's dress up like animals and make masks!"*
Tanya:	*"Let's have rainforest sounds and bring in food that we'd find in a rainforest!"*

The kids excitedly transformed their classroom into a veritable rainforest over the next several days: Classroom ceilings, walls, and floor literally became a rainforest of sounds, sights, and smells. The children found that their ideas were met with an equally enthusiastic response. This, in turn, served as a springboard for a variety of learning activities in math, language arts, science, and social studies. The kids researched selected animals, developed plays, wrote "just-so" stories, and felt an unconditionally warm invitation to be part of an enjoyable learning experience.

ACTIVITY 56: TRIP ACROSS THE UNITED STATES

Grade levels:	4 and above
Time involved:	3 to 5 class sessions (or more)
Organizational pattern:	Kids work in pairs
Teacher's/parent's role:	Guide the activity, provide needed resources
Learning styles:	All can be accommodated

A classroom teacher brings in a set of U.S. highway maps for her children. For several days, they select and "buy" a car from various auto dealership magazines and brochures, and plan a four-week trip around the country (any region of their choice).

Her kids look up the gas mileage for the particular car, compute daily mileage, cost of gasoline per mile (and total cost for entire trip), and driving distances based on miles per hour and stops (gas, food, sightseeing, and so on). They research various states along the route for points of interest, using the classroom's extensive collection of *National Geographic* and *Arizona Highways* magazines, various auto club and travel magazines, travel guides from the forty-nine continental U.S. states and Canadian provinces, and appropriate Internet websites as resources.

Her kids develop an itinerary and write a daily journal of their travels, as well as create colorful posters or brochures of their travels!

ACTIVITY 57: ROLE REVERSAL

Grade levels:	1 or 2 and above
Time involved:	Can vary
Teacher's/parent's role:	Explain purpose and procedure
Learning styles:	Can adapt to any learning style(s)

A sixth-grade math teacher from a rural school district never assigns typical math homework, but rather has kids practice a new algorithm (computational procedure) by teaching the skill or concept to another person (usually a family member or friend). Interestingly, kids become so caught up in playing the teacher they invariably do more problems than normally assigned. (When assigned a conventional fifteen- or twenty-question worksheet, kids often rush through the assignment just to get it finished.) Not only do these kids—as "teachers"—enjoy the role reversal, they become more involved with each problem, and ensure their "student" fully understands the process and has the correct answer before moving on.

The teacher then asks all the children to turn in the lesson sheets they had prepared for their parents, signed by the "students," with the "grade" that was given. Needless to add, the majority of the grades were As, with a few "stray" Bs.

Extender: Although math lends itself best to this particular approach, you'll find that this approach also works effectively with spelling, language arts, and other content areas. Teachers and parents find that their kids invariably have a better grasp of content when they function as a teacher, whether it's with a family member, classmate, or a cross-age tutor.

Although this approach was used in this particular school, it provided a closer homeschool connection, and it's presently used by a number of teachers at many schools.

ACTIVITY 58: CREATIVE BACKTRACKING

Grade levels:	4 and above
Teacher's/parent's role:	Introduce and guide the activity
Learning styles:	All can be accommodated

Invite your kids to become a historical object and write a historical account from the new perspective. One teacher applied this idea to the children in her classroom in a study of the American Revolution. One child became Betsy Ross' needle, another, Ben Franklin's bifocals. Others imagined themselves as John Hancock's pen, Paul Revere's (or Richard Dawson's, who wasn't immortalized by Longfellow) horse, George Washington's boat crossing the Delaware, an East India Tea Company crate of tea at the Boston Tea Party, and even Patrick Henry's tongue! Her kids immensely enjoyed personifying historical items, animals, and even insects (for example, a butterfly at the Battle of Lexington). Their imaginative accounts were wonderful!

Extend this activity by having kids keep diaries or journals, write letters or newspaper articles from the viewpoint of a historical figure, create dioramas or videos, construct a colonial scene, and so forth. The list is endless!

These activities serve as a springboard for further learning and soon her kids become experts about certain people and events associated with the Revolutionary period.

ACTIVITY 59: A GUBBLEBUM TALE

Grade levels:	All
Time involved:	20 to 40 minutes
Teacher's/parent's role:	Guide kids through activity
Learning styles:	Verbal-linguistic, visual-spatial, bodily-kinesthetic, mathematical-logical, intrapersonal, interpersonal

Provide your children with bubblegum and invite them to blow bubbles. Ask your kids to close their eyes and imagine themselves inside their bubbles. Now give your children time to imagine an experience inside their bubbles. Softly ask questions, such as: *How did you get inside your bubble? What are you experiencing inside your bubble? Try to imagine that you are floating and tumbling to and fro in your bubble. Describe to where you would travel if you could travel anywhere in your bubble.*

The imaginative experience lends itself to creative writing and illustrating the adventure, as well as mathematics in determining possible intercontinental mileage traveled, time zones crossed, timelines developed, and the like. (This type of lesson can be extended into a variety of directions, including air pressure and temperature at various elevations and climate zones, or a musical selection, such as *Up, Up and Away,* with lyrics rewritten to describe the adventure.) At the end of the activity, invite your children to share their stories and artwork.

ACTIVITY 60: FRIDAY READ-A-THON

Grade levels:	2 and above
Time involved:	Open-ended time
Organizational pattern:	Flexibility with physical arrangement
Teacher's/parent's role:	Provide resources, guidance
Learning styles:	Verbal-linguistic, intrapersonal, interpersonal

Educators agree that the best way to improve reading ability is simply to read enjoyable books. One classroom teacher of upper elementary level children brings a new selection of interesting paperbacks for kids to read during this reading time. One category is *Adventures: People and Animals;* books in this group include William Armstrong's *Sounder,* Fred Gipson's *Old Yeller,* E. B. White's *Charlotte's Web,* Jim Kjelgaard's *Big Red,* Scott O'Dell's *Island of the Blue Dolphins,* Jean Craighead George's *Julie of the Wolves, Where the Red Fern Grows,* and others. Each child selects a book to read.

Her class often goes outside for a Friday morning read-a-thon. Kids are found leaning against a tree or prone on the ground; some propped against the home or school building, others positioned back-to-back. There are neither disruptions nor behavior problems. Kids are so excited about the books that a two-and-a-half-hour reading period often occurs during which kids are completely engrossed in what they're reading. After lunch, kids briefly share what they read that morning, whetting appetites for future selections.

This technique can be applied to other content areas. For a history class unit on the Civil War, kids immensely enjoy Julius Lester's *To Be a Slave,* Irene Hunt's *Across Five Aprils,* and Paula Fox's *Slave Dancer,* to cite several (all of which are either Newbury Medal or Honor Books). Written in the narrative, these books tend to be more engaging than many history textbooks; therefore, much more of the factual content is absorbed and understood (even with historical fiction!), as well as enjoyed, by the reader.

Read-a-thons are not confined to the upper grade levels. An enterprising country schoolteacher of young children (grades PreK-2) has developed a very creative spider unit that thoroughly engages her children. She has a water tray with two 18-inch upright dowels, spaced twelve inches apart, and connected with a taut line of string at the dowel tips. Gracing the structure is a garden spider that she brought in. Her children maintain written logs of the spider's daily activities, develop geometric spider webs, and read all that they can on spiders. She also incorporates a mini-read-a-thon with her children and brings in spider books, such as *The Very Busy Spider* and *The Itsy Bitsy Spider*, as well as introduces spider songs such as "Teensy, Weensy Spider Went Up the Water Spout."

We need to continually ask ourselves this question: Would we enjoy this learning environment if we were our children? And do we, as teachers and parents, enjoy this now?

Activity 61: Newspaper Shopping

Grade levels: 3 and above
Time involved: Will vary
Materials needed: Writing materials, newspapers
Teacher's/parent's role: Explain and guide activity
Learning styles: Mathematical-logical, verbal-linguistic, interpersonal

In this activity, your children plan a meal and do comparison shopping for the best buys in food. Your kids use a copy of a local paper to compare prices of various grocery market ads and learn to shop wisely.

This is a terrific activity for real-life application of content learning (math, social studies, health), problem solving and group decision making, and cementing of estimating and computational skills. With older children, such concepts as percents involving sales tax and discounts can be compared.

Teacher and parents involving a child in the actual shopping for a planned meal will enhance this activity. In the store, she can compare brands and their prices, as well as compute price per ounce. Making children wise shoppers at a young age is as important as teaching them how to compute.

ACTIVITY 62: BOOKS GALORE!

Grade levels: PreK and above
Time involved: Varies
Teacher's/parent's role: Provide direction and resources (if needed)
Learning styles: Can accommodate all learning styles

There are ways other than the traditional oral and/or written book reports to motivate kids to share an interesting book they've read. A few are listed below.

Have kids:

1. Create a book jacket, complete with inside flap information.
2. Create a very condensed "Big Book" to share with a younger audience.
3. Develop a mural for classroom or home display that depicts a scene from the book.
4. Become a character from the book—represent a character's dress and have the class interview you as the character.
5. Write a script and present a play from a scene in the book. (They can have classmates who have read the book join in the activity.) You may wish to videotape this.
6. Rewrite or add to the ending of the book, or develop a condensed form of the story to fit a contemporary setting.
7. Develop a tape cassette adaptation of the story, with sound effects.
8. Create additional illustrations for the story.
9. Adapt the story to a puppet theater presentation for younger children.
10. Create an "alphabet book" for younger children. On each page, place one letter of the alphabet and then cut out pictures of objects that begin with that letter. You could even have photos of classmates whose names begin with that letter on each page.

ACTIVITY 63: FOLK TALES, FAIRY TALES, AND FANTASIES

Grade levels:	All
Time involved:	Varies
Teacher's/parent's role:	Provide books, guidance, and follow-up sharing
Learning styles:	All can be incorporated

Kids find themselves deeply engaged in imagination: Folk and fairy tales come to life. Such stories attract their fancies and confirm their suspicions and sense of wonder about the world. In fact, there is nothing more enriching to the imagination than folk and fairy tales.

Traditional tales also enable kids to read and hear about human problems and how to go about solving them. Thus, kids realize that nothing in life comes easily, that one must struggle in order to overcome problems and achieve goals.

Such stories generally deal with moral issues and reinforce a sense of right and wrong, which helps teachers and parents teach their children these things. Tales involve good and bad characters. Kids are able to identify with the good characters and reject the bad.

Finally, traditional tales are simply fun! As a magical net, they draw kids into their web of fancy, intrigue, adventure, and delight.

Once a book is completed, your children will enjoy watching the story come to life on video. Most of the books listed below are available on commercial videotapes. You and your kids may wish to create your own video of a scene from the story.

Your children may wish to create puppets and produce a puppet play of one of the stories, or they may wish to weave from their own magical, imaginative threads and create their own story.

There are a number of books with tales from throughout the world for all ages from which to choose. Some are traditional, some are contemporary. A few are listed below:

Folk Tales & Fairy Tales:

Aardema, Verna	*Bringing the Rain to Kapiti Plain*
	Princess Gorilla and a New Type of Water
	Rabbit Makes a Monkey of Kion
	Who's in Rabbit's House?
	What's So Funny, Ketu? A Neur Tale
Allen, Linda	*The Giant Who Had No Heart*
Andersen, Hans Christian	*Fairy Tales (Denmark)*
Arnott, Kathleen	*Animal Folk Tales Around the World*

Bang, Molly	*The Paper Crane*
Collidi, Carlo	*Pinocchio*
Cook, Scott	*The Gingerbread Boy*
DeRoin, Nancy	*Jakata Tales*
Freedman, Florence B.	*Brothers: A Jewish Legend*
Grahame, Kenneth	*The Wind in the Willows*
Haley, Gail	*Jack and the Bean Tree*
Harris, Joel Chandler	*Uncle Remus and His Friends*
Haviland, Virginia	*Favorite Fairy Tales Told in Norway*
	Favorite Fairy Tales Told in India
Holder, Heidi	*Aesop's Fables*
Isele, Elizabeth	*The Frog Princess*
Juo, Louis & Yuan-hsi	*Chinese Folk Tales*
Lamont, Patricia	*The Troublesome Pig*
Lewis, C. S.	*Chronicles of Narnia* (seven volumes)
Mayer, Mercer	*East of the Sun and West of the Moon*
McDermott, Gerald	*Arrow to the Sun: A Pueblo Indian Tale*
	Sun Flight
Milne, A. A.	*Winnie-the-Pooh*
Norton, Mary	*The Borrowers*
	The Borrowers Afield
	The Borrows Aloft
Otsuka, Yuzo	*Suho and the White Horse: A Legend of Mongolia*
Paulus, Trina	*Hope for the Flowers*
Ross, Tony	*Stone Soup*
Selden, George	*The Cricket in Times Square*
Silverstein, Shel	*The Giving Tree*
Steptoe, John	*Mufaro's Beautiful Daughters*
Toye, William	*The Loon's Necklace*
Wildsmith, Brian	*The Miller, the Boy and the Donkey*
Williams, Margery	*The Velveteen Rabbit*
White, E. B.	*Charlotte's Web*
Wyndham, Robert	*Tales People Tell in China*
Yagawa, Sumiko	*The Crane Wife*

ACTIVITY 64: INVITE AN AUTHOR OR ILLUSTRATOR

Grade levels:	All
Time involved:	Varies (most authors and illustrators of children's books are available for an hour or so and can be contacted through a state's reading or library association)
Teacher's/parent's role:	Provide exposure to author's or illustrator's books before meeting the author or illustrator

Excite and inspire kids about literature! One central California teacher discovered that a well-known children's author was speaking at a nearby university. She immediately contacted other teachers, as well as several homeschool groups and families, and then called the author prior to his engagement and invited him to speak to the eager group of children. The combined classroom groups were keenly interested in this author's books and in the author himself. That next week, much to the surprise of the children, this best-selling children's author arrived with a slide projector (with slides of illustrations from a forthcoming book) and captivated his audience for over an hour.

ACTIVITY 65: FOCUSING ON A TEXTBOOK PASSAGE WITH IMAGINATION

Grade levels:	2 and above
Content area:	Any area
Time involved:	Anywhere from 20 to 40 minutes
Organizational pattern:	Group kids in pairs
Teacher's/parent's role:	Guide kids in activity
Learning styles:	All learning styles can be incorporated

Prior to reading a passage from the social studies text, have kids close their eyes for several minutes as you take them on an imaginative field trip to a 1700 colonial schoolhouse.

You're standing outside the schoolhouse. Look carefully at its features. Notice each little detail . . . the door . . . the roof . . . the walls . . . windows.

Walk inside and look around. Take in every detail. Look at where the students are seated. How are they dressed? How do they write? What are they studying? What does the schoolmaster look like? What else do you see in the classroom?

Listen very carefully and describe sounds that you hear in the schoolhouse. Now describe what the classroom smells like. Pick up an object in the room. What did you pick up?

How does it feel to be back in time three hundred years? Note your feelings. How are things different from today? What would you miss from the 2000s? What changes would you anticipate?

After discussing their thoughts and sensations from this imaginative session, your children read a short section in the textbook about colonial schools. They are reminded to use notation (see page 91). When they're finished, they write in their partner journals (see page 94) and share what they found that was new and interesting.

The entire class then shares what they found to be the most interesting facet of a colonial schoolhouse.

Extenders: Applying this concept to the mid-1800s of mid-America, have kids break into small groups to research additional information, construct a prairie schoolhouse to scale, develop a dramatized scene from the era, and so forth.

Read aloud to your class passages from *Little School on the Prairie* or *Sarah, Plain and Tall.*

Prepare cornbread with homemade butter, as well as any other food items that might have been found in those times.

Teach children simple weaving. Bring slates for them to write on.

Play background music from the era.

In short, immerse your kids in the unit. Not only will they have a better understanding of (and relate to) what they're studying, the memory of this learning experience will remain with them.

GUIDING YOUR CHILD'S DISCOVERIES

One of the most important gifts that we can give our children
is to open their eyes to possibilities without limits.

Anonymous

Kids have insatiable curiosities. They question anything and everything. They have a need to know at the very moment and they are not about to be put off. There are some teachers and parents, unfortunately, who stifle curiosity by exclaiming, "Can't you be quiet for once! Would you quit asking so many questions!" Others wisely nurture this quality in their children and provide opportunity and encouragement for further questions.

We need to keep this thought in focus: All the world's most precious treasures *are* in the mind of a child, and it's a wise person who knows how to keep a child's mind active and stimulated. The following activities are but a small sample of many approaches that can be used. (Additional investigative activities are found in the next chapter.)

ACTIVITY 66: DISCOVERERS

Grade levels:	All
Time involved:	Varies
Teacher's/parent's role:	Guide activity, provide necessary materials and access to needed resources
Learning styles:	All can be accommodated

The following are observations of a very effective homeschool teacher and parent:

Jeremy:	*Why does this work that way? Will it work with other numbers?*
Homeschool teacher:	*I'm not sure. Have you tried it with other numbers to see if it works with them?*

(Jeremy tests his theory with other numbers.)

Another example:

Vicki:	*Okay, I see how you got the egg into the bottle, but how do you get it out?*
Parent:	*I'm not certain. Do you have any ideas?*
Vicki:	*Well, besides breaking the bottle or the egg, maybe I could pour vinegar into the bottle to soften the eggshell, then get the egg into the mouth of the bottle and heat the bottom. I remember learning that heat creates pressure and can expand. Do you think it'll work?*

(Vicki finds that it does work.)

Too often, teachers and parents act as custodians of knowledge, who gather important facts and truths, and pour them into the "empty minds" of their kids. But this method simply develops dependent children.

Learning experiences may take a bit longer, concepts may need additional time to develop, yet we must ask ourselves: Is it so important that we spell it out to kids, or, rather, should we simply guide them to reach their own discovery and understanding? The first method often leads to rote, short-term learning; the second leads to understanding and long-term learning.

ACTIVITY 67: ENCOURAGING QUESTIONS

Grade levels:	All
Time involved:	Varies
Teacher's/parent's role:	Set the stage for learning, guide the activity with appropriate questions by both adult and kids
Materials needed:	Varies according to activity
Learning styles:	All can be incorporated

A father of second-grade twins elicits active responses from his children. On one particular occasion, he brought home a variety of small plants—some healthy, others dying or already dead. The father encouraged questions about what plants need for survival and growth, and the afternoon was filled with questions and suggestions. Each child was given a plant, and together both father and twins researched the essential ingredients needed for proper plant care.

This strategy serves as a springboard for further questions. An energetic parent-child dialogue develops, and kids freely involve themselves at greater depths in what is being investigated—whether it's a science activity, historical event, or a current event topic heard on a news broadcast.

ACTIVITY 68: HOW MANY PAPERCLIPS?

Grade levels:	All
Time involved:	Varies
Teacher's/parent's role:	Set the stage for learning, guide the activity with appropriate questions on both adult and kids
Materials needed:	Small cup filled to the brim with water, box of small paperclips, pencil, paper
Learning styles:	Bodily-kinesthetic, verbal-linguistic, mathematical-logical, interpersonal

Give your kids a small cup of water that is filled to the brim, ready to spill over. One cup per team of two children will work well. A small box of paperclips is placed alongside.

Ask individual teams how many paperclips they can place into the filled cup of water without one drop spilled over. Record their "guesstimates."

Instruct them to slowly place one paperclip at a time into the cup. One child will drop the paperclips; the other will record the number of paperclips on a sheet of paper. Roles may be reversed periodically.

Your kids will be amazed as to the number of paperclips that can be dropped into the cup, and they will wonder why the water level appears above the rim of the cup yet does not spill (unless, of course, they place too many paperclips into the cup)! (A small plastic drinking cup can hold approximately 250 paperclips, if not more.)

Extenders: Ask your kids if a paperclip can float, and invite them to try to float one. (If the paperclip is gently placed onto the water surface at the edge of the cup, with the front portion of the paperclip gradually lowered onto the water surface, kids will find that they can float a number of paperclips in the same cup.) Also, ask kids for their observations, such as, "Where do the paperclips tend to move?" "What is causing the bulge in the center of the cup?" "What allows paperclips to float?"

Another related activity is to provide your kids with pennies, a small container of water, and an eyedropper, and again let them work in teams of two. Ask them to guess how many drops of water they can place onto a penny (using the eyedropper) without one drop spilling over. Invite them to experiment with the "heads" side, "tails" side, a shiny penny, or a soiled penny, placing the drops from the inner portion of the penny toward the outside, and vice versa. Now let them share their observations.

(The answer for all activities is *surface tension* provides a seal on top that binds water molecules together. As for the pennies, you may wish to join your kids in the experiment!)

Creative Problem Solving

In order to develop into fully functioning self-reliant adults, kids need to develop effective, creative problem-solving skills as part of their repertoire. Possessing such skills enables kids to intellectually approach and emotionally cope with everyday and challenging problems that arise in life. It also provides kids with a broader perspective. Rather than view only one approach to solving or minimizing a problem, kids learn to defer judgment, brainstorm alternative solutions, and critically assess the merits of each approach. The two activities that follow are but a sampling of the many possibilities that exist.

ACTIVITY 69: STRAW TOWERS

Grade levels:	2 and above
Time involved:	15 to 30 minutes
Materials needed:	Package of colorful drinking straws, masking tape, tape measure
Teacher's/parent's role:	Provide directions (and, if at home, join the activity)
Learning styles:	Bodily-kinesthetic, visual-spatial, mathematical-logical, interpersonal

Provide your children with the required materials and a flat, smooth working surface. The objective is for you and your kids to construct the tallest, self-supporting straw tower that you can. You and your kids have fifteen to thirty minutes in which to design and build the towers.

Not only will kids and teacher (or parent) have fun constructing straw towers, but this activity can also be used as a springboard into basic engineering design-discussing successes of structures, building methods, and team planning.

Variations: You may use spaghetti in place of straws, for variety; however, spaghetti is breakable and can be messy.

Supply your kids with several boxes of flat toothpicks and a bottle of white glue, and challenge them to design and construct toothpick bridges to support the greatest amount of weight. Kids explore different bridge designs that will hold various objects, such as erasers, staplers, then books or heavier objects. Be sure to allow enough drying time for the glue before kids attempt to test their engineering designs.

Activity 70: What Would Happen If . . . ?

Grade levels:	1 and above
Time involved:	10 to 20 minutes
Materials needed:	None
Teacher's/parent's role:	Provide open-ended questions, guide activity
Learning styles:	Verbal-linguistic, visual-spatial, intrapersonal, interpersonal

Open-ended questions are an excellent way to stimulate your kids' creative abilities. Not only will your kids become more fluent (with ideas) by looking for a number of possibilities, but they will also become more flexible in their thinking, original with their ideas, and elaborate with their solutions. Kids love such activities. They can use their imaginations to their fullest extent!

The following questions are a sample of what can be used:

1. What would happen if gravity suddenly stopped every day at noon for exactly five seconds? Make a list. What would be some possible solutions to deal with this problem?
2. What would happen if leaves on trees suddenly stopped falling?
3. What would happen if all the trees in the world were suddenly missing? What would be some possible solutions to deal with this problem?
4. What would happen if everyone in the world looked alike? How would we deal with it?

5. What would happen if all the numerals and numbers in the world disappeared? How would we count and keep track of everything?

6. What would happen if each person could speak only twenty words? Make a list of all the problems that might develop. Think of some solutions. (By the way, which twenty words would *you* select? What was your reason for choosing each of the twenty words?)

7. What would happen if the ice caps at the North and South Poles suddenly began to melt? How might we solve the problems that would develop?

8. If you could do three things to help humanity, what would be the three things that you would select? Describe why each one is important to you.

7

KEY 6: COMMITMENT—HELPING KIDS DEVELOP PERSEVERANCE

Commit your way unto the Lord; trust also in Him, and He will bring it to pass.

Psalm 37:5

GOAL SETTING . . . GOAL ATTAINMENT

So often, kids will start something, yet never finish it, and go to something new. What is needed is a gestalt—that is, a finishing—a completion, of what they had set out to do. What we want to develop within our children is a strong sense of perseverance to complete that which lies before them. And yet we don't want to discourage children by pushing them. The desire must come from within themselves. Also, we must realize that kids may start something they soon discover is not for them. Rather than strongly push them to follow through, we should help them find what they would like to try, keeping in mind that in order to attain anything, it must be done in small, successful steps, and there must be a true innate desire in place.

Young children need short-term goals that are attainable. As they grow older, their goals begin to extend in time and scope; yet again, their goals must be within reach. Only when kids mature and develop a deeper confidence can they set their sights on goals that may appear beyond their grasp. It is then, when they develop the perseverance needed, that they are able to extend their reach, their minds, and their hearts to seek and attain the goals that are before them.

RESEARCH FINDINGS

Studies consistently show that developmentally appropriate, yet challenging learning activities, when combined with an interest in the learning activity, will stimulate children's cognitive abilities, and their brains must literally rise to the occasion, thereby developing even richer dendritical networks. Coupled with this is the development of personal perseverance to see a learning activity to its completion. Learning activities that come too easily do little for cognitive growth. Further, children who do not learn to develop perseverance frequently never develop into lifelong learners or even realize their full potential.

Applying this directly to the classroom or home, while kids are attempting to solve a mathematical problem or a science experiment or write a story, they need to learn that goals are not generally attained on the first attempt. Perseverance is needed. This is where character begins to develop.

Activities that follow are designed to encourage kids to set goals and develop the perseverance to pursue and attain them.

Strategies and Activities

Without a worthy follower, a worthy dream vanishes.

Charles Edwards

Activity 71: Reflections on Goals

Grade levels: All
Time involved: Can vary
Teacher's/parent's role: Join children in activity, guide activity
Learning styles: Intrapersonal, interpersonal

Take a quiet walk outdoors with your children and find a place where each of you can be in close proximity, yet have some privacy. (In a classroom setting during inclement weather, children can find a "quiet" place within the classroom or building itself. Soft music can be played during the activity, if in the classroom.) Find a comfortable place, whether you lie on your back on a flat rock, sit at the foot of a tree or by a pond, or lie on the grass and look toward the sky. For ten minutes or so, reflect on your hopes and dreams, what you'd like to see take place in your life.

Rejoin your classmates and teacher, and share your goals and discuss your feelings about each.

Provide encouragement to each other, as well as continued support, as each one strives toward those dreams and hopes.

ACTIVITY 72: YOU LIGHT UP MY LIFE!

Grade levels:	K-6
Time involved:	20 to 30 minutes
Teacher's/parent's role:	Explain purpose, describe personal example to illustrate directions
Materials needed:	Construction paper (various colors), scissors, tape recording of *You Light Up My Life* (or similar recording), marker or pen, pencil
Learning styles:	Verbal-linguistic, visual-spatial, bodily-kinesthetic, musical-rhythmic, intrapersonal, interpersonal

It is essential for kids to have those *significant* others who have made a positive impact upon their lives, and to realize if it wasn't for the encouragement of these significant persons, kids would not be who they are today.

Invite your children to listen to a tape recording of *You Light Up My Life* and discuss together what the lyrics mean to them. Kids then create the shapes of a candle and flame, using construction paper, pencil, and scissors. On the flame, each child writes the name of a person who lights up her life. On the candle, she writes a sentence describing why she chose that particular person. (As teacher or parent, be sure to join the activity. It's essential that we maintain a sharing relationship with our children.)

Seated together, children present their candles to others before mounting them onto a bulletin board.

Later, each child can give (or mail) her candle to the particular person written about on the candle.

Variation: Play *Wind Beneath My Wings* for your kids and invite them to share who their heroes are—perhaps it's someone who helped them to believe in themselves, or maybe someone who has been a mainstay in their lives.

ACTIVITY 73: BECOMING A HERO OR HEROINE

Grade levels: All
Time involved: Varies
Teacher's/parent's role: Provide resources, guide activity
Learning styles: All can be incorporated

Read with your children some of the stories presented in the previous chapter or from the Bible. Discuss favorite heroes (David, Daniel, Joshua . . .) and heroines (Deborah, Ruth, Esther . . .) with your children. Ask them to define in their own words what a hero (or heroine) is and some of the qualities that heroines and heroes exemplify.

Invite your kids to write a story of a hero or heroine and create one or more pictures to illustrate their story.

Ask your children how they might become heroes or heroines: helping another person or animal, standing up for something they believe in, refraining from fighting or arguing with siblings or friends, giving something special to someone else.

A great source is *My Bible Dress-Up Book* by Carla Williams (ISBN 078143436X). This book provides an opportunity for your child to get involved with the Word of God and fulfill his or her natural curiosity for make-believe with a little assistance. Children can follow simple how-to instructions for making Bible costumes and know the excitement of being David facing Goliath or even Esther saving her people or perhaps Daniel in the lion's den. Your child will have lots of fun learning about the stories of the Bible.

Other art activities are to make papier-mâché models of storybook characters and props, create illustrations for a particular story, or design a mural of a favorite scene.

If your child enjoys creative dramatics, creating a costume and role-playing a particular character provides absolute delight!

The books that are listed on page 100 are but a very small sample of good bedtime reading books for kids. Many of those listed fit nicely into a multicultural gender, providing added enrichment. Perusing children's sections in bookstores or libraries will add to this list. Also, there are periodicals containing information on current recommended children's books, such as *Book Review Digest, Booklist, The Horn Book Magazine, Parents' Choice: A Review of Children's Media—Books, Television, Movies, Music, Story Records, Toys and Games.*

ACTIVITY 75: GROUP OR FAMILY INVESTIGATIONS

Grade levels: All
Time involved: 1 to 2 weeks
Teacher's/parent's role: Guide activity
Learning styles: All can be accommodated

Another family or classroom project is the short-term research project. Children learn the value of patience and perseverance in such an endeavor.

The classroom or family investigation is a short-term research project divided into two phases: preparation and product. Family members or classmates will select and research a suitable topic of interest to all, then prepare a product.

Family or classroom investigation preparation: Family members or the classroom group select an area of interest, then brainstorm possible research topics. The group might select archaeology as an interest area and choose to investigate the Mayan or Aztec civilization. Another possible topic may be advanced agricultural techniques and select hydroponics to study. And still another topic possibility is investigating insects and selecting caterpillars and butterflies.

After the group members have selected and decided upon resources needed, as well as individual responsibilities, group members take one to two weeks to investigate their area of study. The investigation utilizes all possible resources, including field trips!

Group investigation product: Investigative members may select any type of end product (or combination), such as:

1. Display center
2. Family produced video
3. Slide presentation or photo display
4. Model constructed
5. Poster
6. Brochure
7. Computer home page
8. Guest speaking engagement at school or community interest group
9. Mural
10. Scrapbook
11. Photo journal
12. Other

Once the general information of the topic has been shared, the group discusses the project and evaluates what was gained from the investigation, as well as suggestions for future group investigations.

ACTIVITY 76: PASSION AREAS

Grade levels:	All
Time involved:	One week to several months or more (depending upon age and depth of activity)
Materials needed:	Varies
Teacher's/parent's role:	Guide project
Learning styles:	Can accommodate all learning styles

George Betts, in his well-developed book and model, *The Autonomous Learner Model: Optimizing Ability*, discusses *passion areas* and their importance to developing independent learners. A passion area is any area in which a child is or can become completely absorbed. By allowing kids to explore their passion areas, a parent or teacher can use the vehicle as a means of developing learning skills, such as developing research skills in locating information, interviewing experts, organizing information in a meaningful way (such as in a notebook), designing and constructing a display, etc. For kids, the exciting thing about pursuing passion areas is that they not only are immersed in an area of keen interest, but they also have an opportunity to share their passions with others.

For younger children, a scrapbook can be developed from pictures collected. A child interested in red wasps would probably look for a discarded wasp's nest, larvae, and so forth. Your child may wish to make a poster showing wasps at various stages of development, display the materials she has located, and present to family members or classmates her findings.

Older kids may wish to develop a display center or create a brochure or video, develop their own website or even write an article for possible publication.

One parent very effectively channels his eleven-year-old son's interest in chess into various learning activities. Together they've explored biographies of famous chess players and the history of the game, developed mathematical relationships and geometrical principles that apply to the game, incorporated game styles of former players (father and son each selected a particular player) to see how particular strategies interwove, set up "impossible" board situations to see if they could creatively problem-solve the predicament, sculpted playing pieces to fit certain time periods or geographical locales, and even team-wrote a satire involving chess metaphors. It is indeed a wise parent or teacher who can adapt learning activities to a child's passion areas.

Kids have insatiable curiosities, which should not be stifled. All educational psychologists are in agreement that a key to effective learning and personal growth is intrinsic motivation—that the child must see meaning in what is being learned and find personal satisfaction in pursuing those areas of learning that relate to her passion area.

When kids are assigned a particular topic to investigate, the interest may not be there, and the child remains emotionally detached from the topic. However, when the child's own interests are tapped, the child always becomes much more involved and absorbed in the learning process.

ACTIVITY 77: INDIVIDUAL INVESTIGATIONS

Grade levels:	K and above
Time involved:	Varies according to interest level and depth of investigation
Teacher's/parent's role:	Guide activity, ensure availability of resources and materials
Learning styles:	All can be accommodated

Your children individually select a new area in any field that is of interest to them, and they develop a presentation for the family, class, or school. Children can use the group investigation format for preparation and presentation, scaled down, of course, to their individual ability levels.

Modification (age levels 5–7): For very young children, develop a scrapbook with pictures and materials collected. For "nonwriters," written entries can be child dictated/parent transcribed, using a language experience approach. The parent writes exactly what the child shares on a particular picture or collected material, such as a butterfly pupa. The child-dictated/parent-written entries become captions for the pictures in the child's scrapbook. A family presentation can be in the form of a show-and-tell format. (Some children enjoy making a video of their investigation and presenting their discoveries "live" on film!)

For children ages eight and nine, this can be somewhat more sophisticated and include newspaper clippings, magazine pictures, and other assorted material that can provide information on their selected topics. An appropriate presentation can be a product of sorts, accompanied with a brief explanation, and followed by a brief question-and-answer session.

Kids love to be considered experts! This activity will allow them to become one and develop perseverance in the process.

ACTIVITY 79: AROUND THE WORLD

Grade levels: K and above
Time involved: Varies, usually 2 to 4 weeks
Materials needed: Writing materials and art supplies, research materials, computer resources, others as needed for dance, art, music and food
Teacher's/parent's role: Guide school, provide resources
Learning styles: All can be incorporated

Kids are invited to select a country of their choice, create a travel agency, and invite other classrooms or homeschool families, friends, and neighbors to tour their countries. They design travel posters and brochures, develop a one-or two-week itinerary, provide a rate of currency exchange and comparative table of costs for hotels or hospices, resorts, restaurants, points of interest, and compile a small booklet, such as "A Guide to France on Thirty Dollars a Day."

To gather information, kids explore the local city or university library (or explore the Internet), contact tourist agencies, contact appropriate offices of consulate-generals, and peruse travel magazines, to list several possibilities.

At the end of the investigation, they host an international bazaar with a luncheon, crafts, and performances for their guests. Kids dress in native apparel, perform dances and songs from their selected countries, teach recreational activities (such as Stick-and-Ball from Columbia) and art forms (Haiku written and illustrated on rice paper from Japan), tell stories (such as "Why the Sun and Moon Don't Live Together" from Morocco), or take the audience on guided imaginary tours of their respective countries. For lunch, "travel guides" and visitors sample such things as sweet bread (Tanzania), kimchi (South Korea), and chiroset (Israel).

Social studies, math, language arts, science, reading, art, music, recreation, and gourmet cooking are thus combined into a meaningful, integrated learning experience. Kids will spend many hours engaged with this project and will love giving their presentation. This kind of learning experience not only develops an extended commitment to an investigative project, but also builds great rapport between adults and children.

ACTIVITY 80: NATIONAL AND WORLD ISSUES

Grade levels:	8 and above
Time involved:	20 to 30 minutes
Materials needed:	None
Teacher's/parent's role:	Guide activity
Learning styles:	Verbal-linguistic, interpersonal

Discussing contemporary issues is important for kids. The issues presented should be appropriate for the level of the child. What is essential is that kids be encouraged to brainstorm a number of ideas and express their own opinions without teacher, parental, sibling or peer censure, or ridicule. Kids need to develop into independent thinkers, not molded to a teacher's or parent's position on a particular national or world issue. Sometimes kids' responses may be farfetched and lack a logical basis. Regardless of the response, their opinions must be respected.

The following issues lend themselves to open discussion and problem solving:

1. What can be done about saving dolphins from tuna fishermen?
2. What can be done about preventing offshore oil spillage? Who should be responsible for cleanup?
3. Should the California redwoods continue to be cut down for timber? What are some problems that might be involved

in this issue? What about the Brazilian rainforest cutback? Should this be continued?

4. Discrimination by color of skin or religious beliefs still takes place. What can be done to stop discrimination? Is there any way to teach others not to be prejudiced?

5. Should animals be caged in zoos? How could some zoos be better than others about providing a good environment for the animals? Should we encourage game preserves as opposed to zoos?

6. There are many people in the United States and the rest of the world who are hungry and homeless each day. What can be done about this? Locally? By individuals? As a nation?

7. Invite your kids to present their own national or world concerns.

8

IN CLOSING: SOARING AS A BUTTERFLY

. . . then are the children free . . .

Matthew 17:26

I want to take this opportunity to personally share as this book comes to a close.

There's an old saying that comes to mind: *He stands tallest who stoops to help a child.* What we do for the "least" of our kids is what speaks about what we really are deeply within us. I've known teachers who wanted their students to make them look good and these same teachers would literally cringe when they found that there were *special ed* or *at-risk* kids, or kids who wanted more in learning than what they were getting, in their classrooms. What a shame! For it's these very kids who can turn out to be the Albert Einsteins, Mother Teresas, Kathryn Kuhlmans, Jime Escalantes, Bill Wilsons and Billy Grahams of this world, who reach out to make a difference in the lives of others. All they need is an opportunity, and unconditional love and support, and they can be transformed from caterpillars into beautiful, strong butterflies who find their horizons extend as far as their imaginations permit. But, it's up to teachers, parents and others who work with children to make this become a reality.

The highest level of learning arrives when children have a solid foundation of love and encouragement, are self-confident, can enjoy the full expression of their abilities, and experience a "high" with learning and growing. It is in this flourishing of abilities, ideas and creative expression that they begin to soar. Enthusiasm is at its highest. Their sights are set before them, and there is a strong inner resolve to see what lies before them become a reality.

This has been the aim of many parents and classroom teachers: to help children reach this level of learning and become all that they can be. It is the realization and appreciation of who they are, and the awareness of the potentials that exist within them that can be developed to their fullest.

Although this level of learning is wonderful to attain and experience, it is even more beautiful at a higher level. The primary purpose of developing their abilities no longer takes on a self-seeking motive—to bring recognition and profit to themselves—but rather to benefit the lives of others and make a significant contribution to humanity, and to serve God in all that they do. It takes all of us who are willing to make that difference in the lives of kids, and to help prepare them for all that they can become. Only then can our kids truly become butterflies and soar high above, as they reach out to make a difference in the lives of others, just as Stripe and Yellow did in *Hope for the Flowers*.

We are the ones who can help make it happen—the ones who can help provide that hope of a brighter tomorrow for each child. And this is what *Marching to a Different Drum: Successful Learning for All Kids* is all about.

"We Haven't Turned Out Yet"

(from "A Quest of Honor" album)

The other day I heard my Mom complaining to my Dad,
It seemed she's quite certain, that I was turning out all bad.

So that night when she came in to tuck me into bed,
I asked her to sit down a while and this is what I said.

I said, Mom, you do not need to worry; I said, Mom,
you do not need to fret.
Those things you always tell me I never will forget.
Someday I'll be a grownup and you'll be proud of me.
You see I'm still a kid, Mom, I haven't turned out yet.

My Dad was telling Grandpa he's worried as could be,
It seems his heart was breaking, he was so ashamed of me.
And so that night instead of Mom, it was Dad who tucked me in.
I asked him to sit down a while and started with a grin.

I said, Dad, you do not need to worry; I said, Dad,
do not give up on me yet.

That spanking you just gave me I never will forget.
Someday I'll be a grownup, and you'll be proud of that.
You see I'm still a kid, I haven't turned out yet.

A little later that same night I heard both Mom and Dad.
I peeked through the keyhole, they were kneeling by their bed.
With arms around each other, they were talkin' kind of sad.
It seems that they were prayin' for this is what they said.

Lord, we ask you to forgive us; Lord, we're so quick to forget.
We were kids not long ago and we're not grown up yet.
Lord, help us to be kind and not do things we'll regret.
Be patient with us, please, Lord, we haven't turned out yet.
Keep working with us, please, Lord, we haven't turned out yet.

Nutritious "Play Dough"

Your kids will have fun mixing these ingredients! Mix one cup of smooth peanut butter, one cup of nonfat dry milk solids, and one cup of honey. (You may wish to increase the number of cups to accommodate larger class sizes.) Stir until thoroughly mixed. Chill until firm.

Place onto breadboard, or wax paper placed on tabletops, and let your kids create numerals or letters. Although this will have a similar texture to soft modeling clay, it's much tastier and provides a healthy snack!

Alternative: Play dough (purchased in most stores) can be used successfully. It's non-toxic and safe for younger children.

To order additional copies of

Marching to a different drum

Have your credit card ready and call

Toll free: (877) 421-READ (7323)

or send 11.95* each plus $5.95 S&H**

to
WinePress Publishing
PO Box 428
Enumclaw, WA 98022

or order online at:
www.winepresspub.com

*Washington residents please add 8.4% tax.
**Add $1.50 S&H for each additional book ordered.